Decluttering and Organizing

Simple Strategies on How to Declutter & Organize to Free Your Mind from Worry & Simplify Your Life

Madeline Crawford

© Copyright 2019 by Madeline Crawford - All rights reserved.

The contents of this book may not be reproduced, duplicated, or transmitted without direct written permission from the author.

Under no circumstances will any legal responsibility or blame be held against the publisher for any reparation, damages, or monetary loss due to the information herein, either directly or indirectly.

Legal Notice:

This book is copyright protected; it is only for personal use. You cannot amend, distribute, sell, use, quote, or paraphrase any part of the content within this book without the consent of the author.

Disclaimer Notice:

Please note the information contained within this document is for educational and entertainment purposes only. Every attempt has been made to provide accurate, up to date, and completely reliable information. No warranties of any kind are expressed or implied. Readers acknowledge that the author is not engaging in the rendering of legal, financial, medical, or professional advice. The content of this book has been derived from various sources. Please consult a licensed professional before attempting any techniques outlined in this book.

By reading this document, the reader agrees that under no circumstances is the author responsible for any losses, direct or indirect, which are incurred as a result of the use of the information contained within this document, including, but not limited to, —errors, omissions, or inaccuracies.

Table of Contents

Declutter Your Home:

Chapter 1: "My House is a Mess!" (The Home Clutter Problem)

Chapter 2: The Proper Mindset for Decluttering Success

Chapter 3: Overview of the Decluttering Process

Chapter 4: Living Room and Family Room

Chapter 5: Bedrooms

Chapter 6: Kitchen

Chapter 7: Bathrooms and Laundry Room

Chapter 8: Closets

Chapter 9: Storage Room

Chapter 10: Entryways, Mudrooms, and Foyers

Chapter 11: Home Office

Chapter 12: Basement and Attic

Chapter 13: Books and Paper Documents

Chapter 14: Garage

Chapter 15: Dealing with Items You Love

Chapter 16: Decluttering in One Day

Bonus Chapter: Decluttering Before Moving

Conclusion

Declutter Your Life:

Chapter 1: Declutter Your Life - The Starting Point

Chapter 2: Proper Mindset when Decluttering Your Life

Chapter 3: Planning Your Time

Chapter 4: Organizing Family Activities

Chapter 6: Organizing Your Finances

Chapter 7: Decluttering with Others in Your Life

Chapter 8: Freeing Your Mind from Worry, Anxiety, and Stress

Chapter 9: Decluttering in the Workplace

Chapter 10: Freeing Yourself from Digital Distractions and Clutter

Chapter 11: The Simple Lifestyle

Bonus Chapter: Planning Family Recreational Activities

Conclusion

References

Declutter Your Home:

Simple Step-by-Step Home Decluttering Strategies on How to Declutter and Organize to De-Stress and Simplify Your Life

Madeline Crawford

Introduction:

If you have a countertop in your kitchen housing various appliances that you haven't used for months, a pile of mail on the table in your home office, or floor areas that require a lot of skill to navigate through, then you have a problem. Specifically, a clutter problem. Understanding that you have this problem in your home must be the reason why you have picked this book.

Here are some facts concerning the clutter problem:

- According to a study by the Soap and Detergent Association, getting rid of an estimated 40% of the housework required for an average family is possible by removing clutter.
- About 23% of adults are late on their bill payments and are forced to settle the late payment fees due to disorganization according to a study by Harris Interactive.
- A survey of 1,000 American women by OnePoll shows that 10% of these women

experience a feeling of depression anytime they open their closets.

- A LexisNexis study shows that, of the numerous items we own, only 20% of them are put to use.

- A Huffington Post survey indicates that clutter-related worry ranks as the 5th highest trigger for stress in Americans.

To solve the problem of clutter, this book takes a look at the various aspects of clutter and how to go about decluttering. The decluttering process focuses on the different rooms in the home and gives detailed steps on how to declutter each room. You learn how to develop a decluttering mindset which is crucial in achieving your decluttering goals.

As a mother, my house was once a cluttered mess. Clutter in my home kept increasing, not because I wasn't doing my best to organize the home, but because I kept making new purchases without getting rid of the old items. From my perspective, I didn't believe I was doing anything wrong until I enlisted the help of a professional for a day. Within a week, I saw drastic changes in the appearance of my home.

To make progress and achieved the home I desired, I kept doing a lot of research into different decluttering ideas in order to come up with the most effective solution. Through my years spent gaining knowledge and my experience decluttering my home, I have found out a lot about decluttering, from the importance of small wins in decluttering to the KonMari strategy, and many more.

My passion for writing this book is to help individuals, especially mothers, who are in a similar spot as I was a few years ago. As a mother, clutter in your home is not an indication of laziness or lack of effort; it just means it is time to find something that will guide you onto the right path.

There are numerous reasons why decluttering is important. Your home is a reflection of who you are. It is a space in which you should feel safe and comfortable, creating a strategy for the future as well as being productive.

Ensuring that the home is clutter-free allows you to enhance your productivity. It also has health benefits as it provides freedom from stress and anxiety.

Here are the replies from individuals that have applied various decluttering strategies to improve their home and their life:

"My life had been a mess after the loss of my mother. I was keeping all her possessions in the hopes that I would find relief from my grief. In the end, I was doing myself more harm than good. Every time I looked at one of her dresses or shoes, I would instantly remember that I couldn't see her anymore.

The break I desired came in the form of methods to declutter items of sentimental value. I wasn't finding it easy, but I took a step to make digital copies of the possessions that mattered most to me. To ease the process of letting go, I called a friend I knew was into charitable deeds. I had him clear out the storage while I watched. With the items gone, I have no regrets. I simply scroll through my photo gallery anytime I want to recall some memories of the woman I hold dear in my heart." – Jenn

"The idea of decluttering wasn't new to me, but I thought I wasn't making any form of reasonable progress. I searched for a lot of information on how to get through this slump. Of all the articles and books I read, the information that helped me the most was focusing on small wins.

My initial focus was on clutter in the entire home. I hadn't taken time to look at my progress in the rooms I had decluttered. I am a lot more motivated to take an extra step now more than ever." – James, NY

This book will provide all the steps you require to declutter each space in your home effectively. You will also find information regarding the importance of the small wins strategy in becoming an expert on the one-day decluttering process.

Solving the problem of clutter in the home is vital so that you can avoid the many issues associated with excessive clutter. Some common problems include injury from tripping over items and stepping on toys in addition to the embarrassment it causes anytime you have a visitor. Health problems associated with increased clutter in the home also include stress and depression. These are some of the critical things that decluttering can help you avoid.

Why You Should Get This Book

The strategies you are about to read can be implemented by anyone regardless of your profession, age, or amount of time available. There are practical actions that you can do as soon as you complete a chapter to get instant results before you even reach the end of the book. In addition to improving your life through decluttering, this book also gives you many excellent tips to help you along the way.

Chapter 1: "My House is a Mess!" (The Home Clutter Problem)

Chapter 1: "My House is a Mess!" (The Home Clutter Problem)

I was finally done with what I would tag as the worst day of my work life.

Frustrated and angry, I kept replaying the early hours of the day in my head. How did I end up leaving my work documents at home? Why did I have my utility bills and a copy of my tax returns in my bag? These were the thoughts that kept bothering me.

I brushed these thoughts aside as soon as my house came into view. My focus now was on finding my work documents. That was more important at the moment, or so I thought.

On opening the door and stepping into the house, I was greeted by the answer to my questions. My home was a mess. There were large piles of clutter lying around. I hadn't created time to put the house in order for a while.

I had my answer, but where did I put my documents? I kept trying to recall where I placed the documents, but every room I thought of had the same appearance of a cluttered mess. My stress was steadily building. The one place

I hoped to find comfort and peace had the exact opposite effect on my life.

During the search for my documents, moving from one room to the other, I tripped and fell over a stack of books on the floor. I was in a rush, so I didn't take notes. Nonetheless, this was the last straw.

My journey towards making my home a clutter-free zone didn't occur in one night. It was a process that I had to repeat over a few months until I achieved the initial results. The later stages involved actively ensuring that I didn't go back to having clutter around the home.

So, how do you define clutter and decluttering?

Simple, clutter is any object, item, or possession that doesn't offer any useful function despite occupying storage space within the home. In most cases, clutter is often a result of indecision on your part as an individual. It appears in the form of your inability to decide on the right place to keep particular objects, what objects to discard, and which things matter the most to us.

Decluttering, on the other hand, is an action you take in which you rid your home of the clutter that you have accumulated over the past days, months, or years. It involves making tough decisions that can help improve your life and create a permanent turnaround in your home.

The increase in the amount of clutter in the home is not a recent development. It is an increase that has been making steady progress from as far back as the Industrial Revolution. The Industrial Revolution was a turning point in history, which gave rise to the development of factories due to the economic freedom and technological advancements of the time.

Factories provided an opportunity to engage in mass production of different products. This increase in the production of goods led to a drop in the prices of these products. The ultimate outcome was a lifestyle of consumerism in which individuals had the opportunity to buy numerous products with each having unique features, all affordable with the salaries that they earned.

The promotion of socialist values that drove the increase in wealth of the middle class as well as the outsourcing of production processes further resulted in a reduction in the price of goods, making them even more affordable. Thus, people adopted the consumerist lifestyle with open arms.

The effects of this lifestyle remain noticeable in today's society where companies are spending large sums of money on marketing campaigns and adverts to promote the purchase of products. The boost in the number of products being released also means that people keep looking to make the latest purchase of the latest products.

Since consumers usually want to keep up with the latest advancements in technology to avoid being left out, it is easy to find homes filled with clothes, electronics, and other items in good condition that are left unused because they don't match the current societal trends. Accumulation of these items in the home is what results in the development of clutter.

Why the Decluttering Process is Essential

There are numerous reasons why decluttering your home is important. For a quick look at some of these reasons, read on below:

You Create More Space in the Home

Clutter in the home limits the space available in the home. You notice that anytime you try to get around the house, there is always something to impede your movement. These are the effects of having too much clutter around.

Decluttering helps in creating ample space for more valuable objects and activities in the home. Besides the physical impact of clutter in the home, it also affects us mentally. The mental effect of clutter is noticeable in the ease with which you get distracted while working. There are different thoughts that run through your head anytime you see a clutter-filled space while working.

You begin to ponder on things like how to arrange the room, eliminating the clutter, and so on. Decluttering creates space for walking, working, and thinking effectively.

It Becomes Easier to Identify Things of Value

Decluttering is forcing yourself to discard the things you don't need. Once you make up your mind to engage in the decluttering process, you must be selective of things that you keep. There is no room to keep items that you think you will need in the future.

You have to decide whether or not you will read a book that has been lying on your desk for a few months or wear a dress that has been in your wardrobe for the past year. If you decide to discard these items, then it means they were of no value to you from the outset.

You Create a Well-defined Preference

The idea of accumulating various objects and possessions is due to the belief that you need these objects. After making purchases, you find it challenging to make use of these items and keep piling them up in your closet or storage spaces. This includes clothes, shoes, cosmetics, soaps, creams, and so on.

Decluttering will help you find out your preferences. Unlike a cluttered storage space or closet that has numerous designs of clothes, shoes and different brands of cosmetics and soaps, a decluttered home only holds the essential items you need.

This means that the clothes you choose to keep are those that suit your taste, style, and preference. You know more about yourself, such as the materials you love as well as the colors that you fancy.

It Boosts Your Savings

Purchasing and accumulating possessions is one thing, but have you ever considered the cost of owning these items. There are particular objects in the home that need regular maintenance while others cost money to move from one location to another. Decluttering will help you save money on these costs.

It is a Great Way to Earn a Substantial Amount of Money

If you made smart choices during the process of accumulating and purchasing possessions, you have the opportunity to earn a reasonable amount of money when you undertake the decluttering process. Besides donating some of your items, you can choose to sell other items of significant value.

If you are considering putting your house up for sale, it is much easier to execute the sale if the home is decluttered.

It Simplifies the Process of Cleaning

Cleaning is a process that takes a lot of time. The time you spend will double if you have to consider moving clutter from one place to the other before you can clean a particular area. Through the decluttering process, you can rid these areas of clutter for good.

For example, ridding your floating shelf of all the souvenirs and mementos on it means less time spent on dusting.

Freedom to Move Around

The more possessions you own, the more difficult it becomes to relocate. You have to consider how you will pack these items, the cost of transportation, the fragility of the objects, and so on. It also restricts you to a particular size house to ensure there is room for everything you need to move.

Decluttering reduces the amount of stuff you own, and this makes it easy to pack your things and move whenever you want. You will also have an easier time settling into your new home since there are fewer items to unpack and arrange as well as little or no decorations to set up.

The Causes of Home Clutter – And How We Can Avoid It

Stacks of Paper

One major cause of clutter in the home is the accumulation of excess paper. Paper comes in the form of coupons, mail, magazines, and books. Having any form of paper scattered around the home creates clutter.

How to Avoid and Prevent in the Future

Attending to your letters and mail as soon as they come in can help you avoid the possibility of paper clutter in the home. The first thing you need to do is get a recycling bin and place it close to your front door. This is where you immediately dump junk mail.

For those that are of significance, create a filing system to store them neatly.

Old books should be donated or sold to eliminate them from home. You should know that the magazines will keep coming if you still have a subscription. Determine whether there are any magazines that you don't read and ensure you cancel the subscription to these magazines. At this age, you should consider going digital.

Failure to Return Objects to Their Proper Spaces

You can create clutter with things that have value in the home. This is possible if you fail to return these items to their proper position after use.

How to Avoid and Prevent in the Future

Be sure to return each item to its proper position as soon as you are done with it. If your family members are not doing an excellent job with this step, you should encourage them to remove an item or two that don't belong in any room they enter and return it to their appropriate space. Of course, you can try this method as well. Repeat this often, and you can prevent this form of clutter in the future.

Clothes

Severe clutter in the home can also result from how we handle our clothes. The clothes fall into different categories, including used, dirty, and worn clothes. A lot of individuals develop the habit of taking off their clothes and leaving them lying around. You may be one of those individuals that fail to put clothes back into the closet after moderate use.

How to Avoid and Prevent in the Future

The action of leaving clothes lying around after taking them out of the closet may simply be due to lack of space. Create more space by discarding the worn and old clothes in the closet. Also, get over the habit of hanging clothes over the back of a chair when you use them moderately.

Creating a rule that you can only take out new clothing after returning the previous clothing helps. As a result, you only have one set of clothing outside the closet at a time. It is also vital you put your dirty clothes in a laundry basket as soon as you take them off.

Thinking That an Item Will Be of Use in the Future

When you think of the possibility of using an item in the future, you tend to keep it around. This makes the item difficult to discard, and having too many of such items creates clutter. It is common for these objects not to be used for anything until they are eventually disposed of.

How to Avoid and Prevent in the Future

Set a deadline for any item you decide to keep for the future. If there is no need for the item in performing any activity around the home by the set deadline, you must discard the item. You have to be realistic. If the deadline is in six months and you don't use it by this time, what is the possibility you will use it in another six months?

Holding on to Items Due to Cost of Purchase

If you spent a lot of money to purchase the item, it is going to be challenging to get rid of it. The majority of people wouldn't feel comfortable in this same situation. However, having a lot of such items around creates clutter in the home.

How to Avoid and Prevent in the Future

Once you have spent money to purchase an item, holding on to it doesn't mean you get your money back. If the item is not useful, then you can't get value out of it. In the future, you must be intentional when making purchases. Any item you are going to spend a large sum of money to get must offer functionalities that you are sure you require.

An Overview of What this Book Will Cover

In this book, you will find out how to adopt a decluttering mindset and the importance of your mindset in achieving success. This mindset change is also essential for progress in various aspects of your life outside of decluttering. Different decluttering activities you will be implementing are explained, including how to properly donate items in your home.

In the chapters that follow, you will learn about some crucial steps that you can take in decluttering each room within the home. Each room has characteristics that there make it unique from the others, and thus require different strategies. We will also tackle how getting rid of items of sentimental value can be difficult and have included a separate chapter to help you get over this challenge.

For those that plan to move to a new home now or in the future, you will find some useful decluttering tips that can help simplify the moving process. If you are not moving anytime soon, you can still make a note to refer to this book when the opportunity to move knocks on your door.

Your Quick Start Action Step:

If your goal is to declutter your home, then it is vital you include it in your schedule. When you have it in your schedule, you start making plans towards completing it. Include your next decluttering session in your Google Calendar to ensure that you get constant reminders. This is a small action that you can take for success in decluttering and other aspects of life.

Chapter 2: The Proper Mindset for Decluttering Success

Chapter 2: The Proper Mindset for Decluttering Success

As individuals, we all have goals or objectives that we plan to achieve sooner or later. Notwithstanding, not everyone will achieve the goals that they have set their sights on. So, what differentiates those that are successful in achieving their goals from those that are not?

The difference in their level of creativity, risk-taking, and intelligence doesn't correctly explain why some people accomplish their goals while others fail. The simple answer is a difference in the mindset of these two separate groups. Those that reach their goals are the individuals that have adopted the right mindset for achieving these goals. The other set of individuals aim for a new goal without making a mindset change.

Now, what is a mindset?

A mindset refers to the various ideas, assumptions, beliefs, and methods that shape the thinking and way of life of an individual. A person's mindset affects how that individual interprets and responds to a situation as well as how they make decisions.

As with a goal you intend to achieve, you need a mindset shift to be successful in decluttering. As a process, it differs significantly from an easy fix to your problems, and you need to understand that it will take a bit of time to reach the results you desire. Due to the time it takes, developing a new set of beliefs is the only way you will be able to see the process through to the end.

Your ability to recognize and accept this fact will be essential in achieving your decluttering goals. There are other things you need to understand about the mindset before we can go over the steps you can take to develop this new mindset that will be beneficial to you.

The research into the relationship between mindset and success by Carol Dweck, a Stanford psychologist, gives a lot of information on the importance of your mindset. A person's mindset can be classified into two main categories, the growth mindset, and the fixed mindset. Knowing the category under which you fall will assist in making the mindset shift you need.

Individuals that have a growth mindset are those that are of the opinion that their basic qualities, abilities, or traits such as intelligence have room for improvements through their hard work. Others with a fixed mindset believe that these qualities or attributes are unalterable, devoid of any possibility of developing further.

The individuals that need a bit of a push are those who have a fixed mindset. It is crucial these individuals learn that there are ways to reshape their thinking. In developing a decluttering mindset, there are specific steps that you can take regardless of your perspective.

These steps are as follows:

1. Accept the Voice of Your Mindset

Your mindset affects your decision-making process. The decisions you make are usually communicated through a voice in your head. It is through this voice that your mindset becomes evident.

Do you consider yourself talented enough to achieve this goal? What will others say if you fail? These are some of the things your mindset will communicate through this voice. All these come during times when you are undertaking a new project.

The phrases change when you are unsuccessful in your undertaking. They take a demeaning tone. You could hear your inner voice say, "You wasted so much time decluttering, but your home is still a mess, that's why you need the help of professionals."

If you continually hear negative phrases from the voice, then it means that you have developed a fixed mindset. It undermines your abilities and makes you believe that you should only try to achieve goals that are within your current level.

2. Understand that You Have a Choice

When you give in to the voice, you give up every chance you have to make progress. Know that there is always a choice available to you. Choice represents the way you decide to interpret a situation, criticism, challenges, and setbacks.

You accept that the insufficiencies of your abilities or talents the moment you start interpreting your challenges or setbacks through a fixed mindset. In the interpretation of the growth mindset, your interpretation of a setback is that you should further develop your talents, put in more effort, and adopt a new strategy.

3. Make a Conversation

The voice of your mindset becomes a loose cannon if you fail to respond appropriately. Your responses should indicate the errors in the assumptions of this voice. Your answer must also reflect that you believe in your abilities.

Your response should consist of you reassuring yourself, and you can make it as cheeky as you want. Here are some examples of what a fixed mindset says and how to respond using a growth mindset:

- The fixed mindset tells you, "You don't have the talent, don't try it."

- You respond, "My talents may fall short at this moment, but I will put in a lot of effort towards personal development."

Here is another typical example that you have undoubtedly heard at least once in your lifetime:

- "If you fail now, you will remain a failure forever."
- Your response should be, "Failure paves the road to success."

4. Take Action

Thoughts remain just that – thoughts. It is how you decide to implement these thoughts that matters the most. Now, from the previous steps you have taken, you have created a new script that meets your preferences. It is now time to take action following this new script.

The idea is to practice the new thoughts you have come up with. This is the only way you can determine the effectiveness of your new mindset. Never limit yourself to just reconstructing the negative thoughts in your head. There must be something to show for the changes you have made.

5. Include the Keyword of the Growth Mindset

The growth mindset is all about making positive changes that will take you higher than your current level. It means that a growth phrase is an indication of the progress that you intend to make soon. So, how do you indicate this intention in your phrases?

Simply adding the word, "Yet," to your phrases shows that you have the intention to work towards this goal. It provides the motivation you need to achieve what you say. Using this word, you can easily convert the statements of a fixed mindset to those of a growth mindset.

For example, you can say, "I haven't started decluttering, yet." It means you are training yourself on how to declutter and will be undertaking the process soon.

Benefits of a Mindset change

There are various reasons why you should change your mindset. A number of these reasons relate to your success as an individual. Here are other benefits:

- It promotes persistence and resilience.
- You start to see your limitations not as a hindrance but as opportunities to develop yourself further.
- You have a better handle on any setback.
- You develop a positive attitude towards life.

Your Quick Start Action Step:

The steps to develop a new mindset need to be practiced frequently until they become a part of you. You can schedule a time in the morning or in the evening to perform these steps. Meditating on these steps can also be of significant help.

Chapter 3: Overview of the Decluttering Process

Chapter 3: Overview of the Decluttering Process

In this book, the approach to decluttering has been made as simple as possible to ease the reader into the process. This approach combines the implementation of the small wins strategy in different parts of the home with later advancing to a one-day decluttering session.

The small wins strategy is the main focus of this book since it is the simplest way for anyone to get a proper handle on the decluttering process. In the following chapters, you will learn how to focus on a single room to perform a deep-purge decluttering process.

The one-day cleaning session is a more advanced approach that requires the individual to know a lot about the decluttering process. The skills required are all developed through the small wins strategy, and therefore, it is not an approach to just jump into during the early stages of the decluttering process. In this session, the entire home is decluttered in a single day.

The small wins strategy is one that focuses on smaller parts of the big picture. It is a strategy that becomes vital when looking at the big picture that can hinder your opportunity to make progress. A small win is defined as an objective or goal you achieve that is of minor importance.

Despite being of minor importance, it usually offers motivation to get more work done. As a result, you can perform several small tasks to attain several small wins. By achieving the small victories on a path to a more significant success, the significance of these small wins increases as soon as you complete the main goal.

How to Declutter Your Home When You Are Overwhelmed

Before you start decluttering, and sometimes during the process, you might suddenly become overwhelmed with how much clutter you have to work through. This feeling can make you stop dead in your tracks and makes it difficult to make any progress. In such situations, it is important that you make things as simple as possible.

To start decluttering and overcome the feeling of being overwhelmed, follow these tips to simplify things:

- Choose just 10 minutes of the day to declutter a small area.
- The area you select might be a countertop, shelf, or closet.
- Quickly gather the items creating clutter into a single pile and start picking items from the pile randomly.
- Do I genuinely love this item? Is this something I use frequently? Is it of any use in the home? These are questions that, if answered honestly, will help you identify the real clutter in your home.
- For items that you respond no to, sort them into different labeled boxes. Some items can be given out to someone you know, others recycled, and the rest donated.
- The items you keep are those that you love and those that you use frequently.
- As soon as the timer hits 10 minutes, stop for the day and continue the next day.

The idea of creating just 10 minutes a day to

perform decluttering will make it less overwhelming during the early stages. As a result, you look forward to the next day when you can pick up where you left off.

Getting started has been simplified, but it is also important that you create a simple strategy to keep you going. Some tips that you can implement are as follows:

- Continue the process of decluttering in short time bursts.
- The short time frame doesn't give room for perfection, so avoid it. You can always return another time to declutter more.
- Talk to friends to find out which items you can give to them.
- The boxes labeled donate or recycle should be moved to your trunk as soon as they are filled so you remember to get rid of them properly.
- Invite someone you trust to assist since it can be challenging to make sound judgment when it comes to getting rid of your possessions.

- Items that you think you may need should go into a box labeled "maybe". On this box, also include the date you put the items into the box. Any item that remains in the box for at least six months should be discarded.

The free space you create after decluttering can also serve as motivation to keep moving forward. Take some time to take in the view, enjoy it, and get attached to this sort of simplicity in your home.

Donating Items You No Longer Need

When you decide to declutter, it is challenging to accept that you will be throwing items in the trash. It is more challenging when the items in question are those that you feel are valuable despite being useless in your home. To change your views to a more positive perspective, it is crucial you consider donating some of the items that you don't think should be thrown out.

There are different ways to donate items, including giving to people around you who are sure to value these items. Regardless, not everything will find a home among your immediate circle of friends or family members.

When you decide to donate, knowing some of the places that accept these donations can be very helpful. There are also specific tips on how to make the donation more appealing to those that need it. This section focuses on certain items that you can donate regularly.

Clothes

A lot of people spend large amounts of money to acquire clothes, so it is understandable when they find it difficult to let go of them even though they are not in use. Giving your unused clothing up for the right cause should offer the motivation you need.

You can keep a special box or donation bag to stuff with clothes you no longer use. Once the bag is full, look for a charity you love and make a donation.

You can visit any of these places to donate your clothes:

- Salvation Army International
- Goodwill Clothing & Donation Centers
- Vietnam Veterans of America

A simple step you can take is to clean the clothes before making a donation. Remember that someone, somewhere, will be smiling thanks to your act of goodwill.

Books

The books you must donate are those that you are sure you are not going to read. It is essential you give them out so they can make their way to homes where they will be of actual value. You should check between the pages of these books to make sure you didn't leave any paper or notes behind before donating them.

Some places you can donate books include:

- The local library
- Operation Paperback
- Access Books
- Schools in your community

Books are easy to pack for donations; one good way is to place unused books in a box. To ensure you make the donation, don't move this box back into a storage area but take it directly to your car as soon as it is full.

Old Cell Phones

The common step people take in getting rid of cell

phones is to put it in a drawer or box and store it away. These phones are usually forgotten and only make an appearance during the decluttering process.

To provide value to others in need, check out these donation centers:

- American Cell Phone Drive
- ReCellular
- Cell Phone for Soldiers

Remember to clear your personal data before giving out your old cell phones.

Tools

You are likely going to have lots of tools that are due for donations. We commonly purchase tools for a specific project that then become useless once the project is complete. Rather than letting them gather dust and take up space in your home, you can donate these tools.

Packing your tools for donations is quite straightforward since most of these tools usually come in boxes. Find a box to pack those without one.

Construction-focused charities like Habitat for

Humanity will be willing to accept these donations.

Computers

Just because a computer is old doesn't mean it is not in good enough condition for use. If you want to make an impact, your old computers can be put to good use in local libraries and schools within your community.

Unless you engage in a computer exchange program to get new computers, you can donate your old computers to these schools and libraries. It is essential you wipe the computer hard drive before making a donation. You can't count on someone else to do the right thing when they find the information you leave behind.

Furniture

The furniture in your home includes some of the items that are always useful to someone else. Recycling furniture is something that happens only on rare occasions, so there is always a need for donated furniture. Check the furniture for nails sticking out, clean, and dust it before making your donation.

Places that accept furniture donations include the

following:

- Operation Homefront
- Furniture Banks
- Salvation Army

Linens

Linens are items that you can choose to donate along with the various clothing items in your home. If you are an animal lover and decide to donate your linens separately, you can make your animal friends happy by donating to an animal shelter. They are essential for use in bathing animals and making bed linings.

Make a call to the local shelter to ensure they are accepting linens before making the trip. Also, wash the items before donating them.

Kitchen Appliances

Kitchen appliances usually occupy a lot of space in the kitchen. This can become a clutter problem when they are not in use. It is an excellent idea to give away the appliances that you no longer use.

If you decide to donate rather than recycle these

appliances, you should make sure you get the cord and other attachments that go along with the appliance to make it useful to whoever receives it.

Cars

If you know the money doesn't matter to you, then you can choose to donate your old cars rather than have them recycled or sell them. In addition to the good you are doing; a tax write-off is a benefit you enjoy from this action.

You can look to these areas to make a car donation:

- Car Talk Vehicle Donation Program
- Car Donation Center

It is necessary to get the car properly cleaned before making the donation. This also gives you the opportunity to find documents and receipts that contain information you don't want to expose.

Your Quick Start Action Step:

Take your first step towards decluttering by engaging yourself in the decluttering of a small space using the small wins strategy. You should also try to implement the various tips given for donating some of your items.

"Declutter Your Life: Simple Decluttering Strategies on How to Declutter and Organize your Life to Free Yourself from Worry and Enjoy Stress-Free Living" is another book by me that gives you more information on how to build a lifestyle focused on decluttering. For those who have a desire to create this sort of lifestyle, you can find the book on the online store.

Chapter 4: Living Room and Family Room

Chapter 4: Living Room and Family Room

Depending on the size of the home, it is common to have either both a living room and family room or just a living room. Larger houses with enough space to spare usually make this distinction while other, smaller homes opt to make efficient use of space by combining the living room with the family room.

In homes where these rooms are separate, the living room has a more formal design while the family room is informal. The formal model of the living room makes it an excellent place for receiving any guests that visit. Regarding its location, it is typical for the living room to be the first room that anyone who enters the house steps into. As a result, there is no need for visitors to get too far into the house to hold a conversation.

The family room is a more informal set-up that is frequently accessed by family members. In this room, you find various items like the television and game consoles that make it the right location for entertainment and other activities like studying and reading. In addition to the comfortable design that promotes social interactions and relaxation, it is also the right place for kids to play around. Since most home designs place the family room close to the kitchen, parents can monitor the kids while they work.

Since all the family members make use of these rooms, it is a challenge to keep them clutter-free at all times. Regardless, you first need to eliminate the most significant sources of clutter in these areas to make progress. Clutter will make it very difficult for these spaces to offers a spot for relaxation to any member of the family.

Steps to Take

1. Purge Items That Shouldn't Be in the Space

There are various things that we keep in these rooms that are out of place. Your paperwork, exercise equipment, unused toys, ornaments, and decorations. These are just a few of the items creating clutter in these rooms.

The first step in decluttering is to purge these items. This step is simple to implement and reduces your workload as you progress with the decluttering process. As a space for relaxation, it is common for members of the family to enter these rooms with items that they can use in relaxing. However, the family member should take these items back to their proper location when they leave.

2. Create Additional Storage

While there are lots of items that you shouldn't keep in these areas, some items must remain here. For such items, having designated storage is essential in reducing the clutter they create. Examples of these items include toys, books, blankets, remotes, and video games.

Vertical storage is an option that you mustn't overlook. You can start by installing shelves that will be useful in storing your entertainment devices like DVDs and video games. A bookshelf is also an excellent addition that can store your books, magazines, and office supplies in a neat and organized manner depending on how effectively you utilize it.

For the toys, you may look to save money

since there is probably a toy box in each child's bedroom. In actuality, having a smaller toy box in the living room will save you from the noise and pain that you experience when stepping on different toys. The toys you keep in this box are those that the kids frequently use anytime you need them around for close supervision.

Creating a clutter-free space is about making the most of anything you own. You can do this by investing in storage ottomans. These function as footstools or stools while still offering internal storage. They are useful in keeping things like magazines and remotes out of sight.

Remote controls and toys often get broken. It is vital you discard these broken items quickly.

3. Go Minimalist With Your Decoration

An excellent way to create clutter in the living room is through your decorating strategy. Decorations that creates clutter include hanging pictures, shadow box art, and excess couch pillows. The stacked books trend is also a decorating style that builds clutter.

A simple action you could take is removing a number of pillows. You should also install floating shelves. These are useful in arranging your pictures and other mementos. You can, of course, donate or re-home decorations that you believe fail to add enjoyment to the space.

4. Decide How You Will Eliminate Items of Value

Some items that create clutter are still of value. In this case, you need to implement a strategy to either donate or sell these items. If you have a collection of DVDs, books, or CDs, you can give them to someone who needs them or sells them to those willing to pay for them.

The contents of DVDs and CDs vary from movies and videos to music and audiobooks. To ensure you don't have any need to retain these items, convert the contents to a digital format. The benefit of this action is to minimize the need for more shelves.

5. Clear Wire Clutter

An entertainment center is an integral part of these home spaces. The problem with the setup is the level of clutter the wires produce. Cord management is an important activity that will help rid the home of this problem. There are numerous steps you can take towards decluttering your cables.

Feeding wires through the wall is one of the simplest methods to rid the cable clutter in the home. Nonetheless, it may not appeal to you as an individual. Although not the best option, you can use the option of covering wires with furniture to clear the visual clutter.

Clearing out cords is not a realistic option so you must come up with creative ways to keep them out of sight. Some excellent choices include the use of area rugs around areas where the cord clutter is focused. Another option is to get a box, container, or basket that you can put the excess lengths of cord in. Matching this container or box to the living room décor will make it more visually appealing.

The last option you have is limit the length of cables and cords you use in setting up your entertainment systems. If the wires are too long, it increases the difficulty you will have in managing the clutter they create.

6. Furniture

This is vital in beautifying your living/family room and making it comfortable for anyone that intends to relax. Besides the beauty, you must also consider the size of the furniture you fit into these rooms. These are usually the items that create the most clutter in the home.

During the selection of furniture, you should pick sizes that don't make the rooms feel overloaded. You should also consider the use of floating shelves to improve airflow and reduce ground clutter. Remember, don't install excess.

Your Quick Start Action Step:

The living room or family room has a lot of open space that you can declutter with ease. Simply go into the room with a box and a trash basket for a quick declutter. The box will be used in packing items that don't belong in the room while the trash basket is for items that need to leave the home. You can do this in 20 minutes and organize the room within 10 minutes.

Chapter 5: Bedrooms

Chapter 5: Bedrooms

The bedroom is a home space for relaxation and recovery of energy after a stressful day of work. To ensure you enjoy your period of relaxation and recovery, it is essential that the bedroom is free of clutter. Despite the need for a clutter-free bedroom, there are various reasons why clutter piles up in this room.

The decluttering strategy that will be of great benefit when working on the bedroom is the four-box method. In this method, you need to get your hands on four boxes that will each serve a unique purpose as you work through the clutter in the bedroom. The labels on each box are as follows:

- Put Away: These are items that are out of place in the bedroom. Any item that has its appropriate storage like a cup that should be in the kitchen and documents from the home office all go into this box.
- Donate/Sell: The items that make their way into this box are those that are no longer of use in your home. Although you don't need them, these items still retain their value. To

make the most of the value they offer, you can decide to either sell or donate these items. Selling gets you a little cash while donating helps those in need.

- Storage: Some of the things creating clutter in your room are things that you don't use often. Pile up this box and move it to your storage room once it is fully packed.

- Trash: In reality, this box is a trash can. Items that are damaged beyond repair and without value are thrown into the trash for proper disposal.

Engaging in The Process

The steps you should take when decluttering the bedroom are given below:

1. Take Out Items and Group Them Into the Boxes

As mentioned earlier, you are using the four-box method to enable the effective decluttering of your bedroom. You need to take out everything that is in your bedroom to have a proper look as you sort through these items.

The easiest items to identify are those that are going into the trash. Items like broken ornaments, damaged clothes, and old shoes should be discarded.

Separate items that you need to take to your storage space. These items are also quite easy to identify. For a simple tip, any item that you haven't used in the last six months should go into the storage box. These are additional items creating unnecessary clutter in the bedroom.

You are sure to find items in your room that are suitable for donating and those that will fetch a reasonable price if you decide to sell them. These items go into the donate/sell box. Here you put things like books and clothes that you know are still useful, but you won't be needing for a long time. This action helps you make the most of your possessions rather than letting them get damaged.

2. Clear the Clutter on the Nightstand and Other Flat Surfaces

The clutter that builds up on your nightstand and other flat surfaces in the home can consist of decorations, books, pens, tissue boxes, and so on. Get to work on these items immediately to get rid of a massive amount of clutter.

The box with the 'Put Away' label is useful at this stage of the decluttering process. Mail and paperwork from your office should go here along with books that you have completed. These items have their appropriate storage spaces within the home so you can take them back after decluttering the bedroom.

Taking out items for recycling is another excellent step to rid the room of clutter. These items include your dried-out pens, old chargers, and tissue boxes. Small objects like this can pile up if you don't take swift action to eliminate them.

The items discussed above are frequently observed on your nightstand. So once you've tackled them, it is time for other flat surfaces in the bedroom. Certain surfaces may be impossible to completely rid of clutter. In such instances, make sure you arrange objects in moderation.

There should be a limit to the pictures, decorations, and lamps you have in the bedroom. A single lamp on your nightstand or dresser can function effectively when you need to read a book. A good action plan is to ensure that each surface in the bedroom doesn't contain more than five items.

3. Tackle the Drawers in the Room

A vanity table or bureau in your bedroom will usually contain drawers that hide a lot of clutter. Take your time in going through these drawers. You mustn't rush the decluttering process.

If you are taking time to declutter, you can avoid the urge to hide more clutter inside these drawers. The simple phrase, out of sight, out of mind, applies to this situation.

As you work your way through each of the drawers, remove the items in each drawer and sort through them. Items that are going back into the drawers should be folded and well organized. Those that are leaving should be put in the donate/sell box. Others go straight into the trash. Questions you can ask yourself to simplify the separation process are as follows:

- Did I make use of it in the last six months?
- Should it be in my bedroom?
- Will it be of value if I donate it?

The answers you give for each question will determine whether you want to donate, discard, sell, or put away the item. After separating items into boxes, you have to return whatever is left into the drawers. Small containers and dividers can help organize the drawer into compartments — these help in keeping similar items in the same partition.

4. Seasonal Items

Decorations, beddings, and clothing that are only useful in a particular season should be kept out of sight to avoid creating clutter. These objects will not be used for months, so is there a need to have these items lying around in the bedroom?

Excellent decluttering actions you can take for such items is to find a cloth bin, comforter bag, plastic, or space-saver bag to fit in these articles. Once you have them in a proper form of storage, find a space to keep them. Under your bed is a great place to store these items since you won't be needing them for a while.

5. Take Out Furniture You Don't Need

Your bedroom is for one sole purpose, and that is for recovery from the day's work. What this means is that the furniture you have in this space should only be the essentials you require to rest and prepare for the day. It is time to identify the furniture that meets these requirements and take out the rest.

If you want to enjoy a period when you can relax and recharge, then having a work desk in your bedroom won't do you much good. When you turn over, and you see a desk stacked with paperwork reminding you of unpaid bills and uncompleted projects, your chances of getting a good night's rest decline.

The size of the furniture is also an important aspect to consider. The smaller the furniture, the more space is offered and the less-cluttered the bedroom appears. It gives you additional floor space for movement.

6. Kids Toys

If you are thinking of piling up the kid's toys in a closet, then you are robbing yourself of valuable storage space in the home. The toys can fit into a bin, basket, or toy chest – a product that was designed solely for this purpose.

As you keep purchasing new toys and piling them up in the home, you notice that, in addition to clutter, you are quickly running out of storage space. A toy chest cannot serve as a great decluttering tool if you end up stacking multiple chests in the room. The toy chest running out of space is a clear sign that it is time to dispose of some toys.

Kids can be very observant when it comes to their toys, but that doesn't mean you can't cleverly discard some of these toys. You can start by removing a few toys and see how they react over the next week. If there is no reaction, then you can donate or discard these toys. Repeat the process until you have a manageable number of toys left. Or get the child involved in the decluttering process themselves.

7. Clean Out Your Closet

The closet is an essential architectural addition in the bedroom. It is crucial to the proper organization and arrangement of clothes and shoes in the home. It can also be one of the places where you keep a lot of clutter in the bedroom.

The clutter that develops in the closet is often due to the excess clothes and shoes you possess. Besides the clutter issue this excess causes, you also have to deal with the problem of selecting clothes to wear daily. You should reduce the number of articles of clothing in your closet to make things easier.

Simple steps you can take include donating clothes and shoes that don't fit or throwing them in the trash depending on the state of the items. The organization of the closet is also a crucial part of the decluttering process. More on this will be discussed in a later chapter.

Your Quick Start Action Step:

First, create a schedule and plan out the day it is most convenient to declutter.

If you want to declutter the kids' room quickly, simply get rid of the toys on the floor that make it difficult to walk with ease. This is often the real cause of clutter in your children's bedroom.

For the adult's bedroom, clear the top of the dressers and nightstands while packing the dirty clothes in a basket and other items that don't belong here in a box. Remember to make the bed during the process to give the bedroom a great appearance.

Chapter 6: Kitchen

Chapter 6: Kitchen

Most of the activities in the home take place in the kitchen. Depending on the layout of the house, the kitchen will be one of the areas that you can easily access from the living room or family room. Since it is where you install your refrigerator, you can expect a lot of traffic into the kitchen.

This high traffic makes the kitchen a magnet for clutter in the home. Clutter often appears in the form of personal belongings left behind by family members, dishes, paperwork, and mail. It is also quite common to find several appliances on the kitchen countertops. Besides, this is where you drop your grocery bags and start distributing items after going shopping.

Due to the various functions it offers as well as the numerous storage spaces in the form of cupboards, refrigerator, and pantry, it is essential that you declutter your kitchen regularly. Surface decluttering is usually quite straightforward since you are going for items on the counter, but you need to go a bit further when you decide to do a deep purge declutter.

Considering the size of the kitchen, the best

strategy you can apply is the divide and conquer decluttering strategy. This strategy allows you to focus on one storage area of the kitchen before moving to the next. In the topics that follow, we will take a look at how to declutter the kitchen pantry, refrigerator, cupboards, countertops, tools, and under the sink. So, let us get started.

1. Decluttering Your Pantry

The pantry is a cupboard in which you store provisions, food, cleaning chemicals, or beverages in the kitchen. In some homes, the pantry is the same as a cupboard while it is separate in others. It is easy to gather excess items in the pantry when you purchase new stock of something without checking what you have left.

Here are some simple steps you can take to declutter the pantry:

- The first step is to eliminate excesses from the pantry. An easy way to determine what items you need dispose of is to identify those that are beyond their expiry date. You should also check through the items inside the pantry to find and throw out those that have been infested by pests.

- If you want to use the pantry solely for food and beverages, then you need to take out any other items like cutlery sets, cups, and so on.
- Separate the items such as spices, ingredients, and food that you are sure you won't use. Some baking spices are common culprits in this case.
- Foodstuffs that are not expired but will not be used in the home should be donated. Visit a food bank to give out these items so they can serve those in need.
- Learn to combine similar items into the same package or use mason jars. Mason jars are excellent for storing spices and cereals to reduce the number of containers you have to organize in the pantry.

2. Decluttering Tips For the Fridge

The fridge is an integral part of your kitchen. It is where you store leftovers and fresh food to prevent them from going bad. It is quite common to forget certain items you store in the fridge if you don't need them for a long time. These items are a part of the reason why you must declutter your fridge.

For steps to take in decluttering your fridge, read on below:

- Remove all the items in the fridge to start the decluttering process.
- Once emptied, ensure you clean the fridge properly.
- Look for food items that have gone bad, including vegetables, fruits, and leftovers in the fridge since it is possible that these items made their way to the back as you added more things into the fridge, making them difficult to see.
- Empty the fridge by throwing out food items that you don't enjoy using

along with spreads, condiments, and dressings that are expired.

- You should also extend this process to food items or ingredients that you only need for a once in a year recipe. These are likely to expire before the next use so make sure you toss them out.

- If you have an excess number of the same foodstuff such as baked beans or ketchup, you can give some out to others to reduce the level of clutter in the fridge.

- Implement the use of plastic or glass containers in storing leftover food in the fridge. These containers offer a see-through feature that makes it easy to identify the item inside and are also durable.

3. Decluttering Your Kitchen Tools

Handheld tools that serve various cooking and food preparation functions are referred to as cooking tools. It is easy to have an excess number of these items since they are small and very affordable.

Other small electrical appliances and gadgets such as handheld electric mixers, timers, and thermometers also fall within this category. There are specific steps that you can follow to declutter these tools effectively:

- First, remove items that don't belong in the storage space of your utensils. Depending on your kitchen arrangement, these may be cups, plates, or gadgets from another room.
- Get rid of tools that are missing a part and those that are broken.
- Using your cooking habits as a guide, identify the gadgets and utensils as well as the frequency with which you use these items in a day. This approach helps determine the essential number of these tools that need to be available for use before the next wash.
- Gadgets and utensils that you don't use regularly should be donated. Don't try keeping that juice extractor for another six months in the hopes you'll finally use it.

- Reduce the number of serving utensils in the home if you don't get visitors often. Four soup ladles may not be necessary and will end up creating clutter.

4. Decluttering Under the Kitchen Sink

The space under the sink is where most people store their cleaning supplies. It often accumulates clutter because, despite buying more items, some products under the sink rarely get used. Since it is usually out of sight, it is more challenging to keep track of what you have.

To clear the clutter under your kitchen sink, you can follow these steps:

- Clear out and avoid buying single-use products like descalers and specialist drain cleaners.
- Replace the use of window cleaners, oven top cleaners, cream cleaners, etc. with the use of microfiber cloths.

- Get rid of highly toxic cleaners that are harmful to pets and kids.
- Shift to the use of reusable cloths and get rid of the pile of disposable scrubbers and cloths under the sink.
- Specialist laundry products should be eliminated from the home. Instead, opt for gentle laundry liquids.
- Discard any item that you haven't made use of in the last 12 months.

5. Decluttering the Cupboards

Since the kitchen usually contains a large number of items, it is common to have all your various cupboards full of different things, including foodstuffs, canned products, dishes, appliances, and so on. It also means you need to declutter the cabinets from time to time. Some easy steps you can take are as follows:

- Pull out all the items in a cupboard.
- Take stock of all the things you pull out and then inspect each item.

- During the inspection, identify items that are expired so they can immediately be thrown away.
- Separate the items that you don't need any longer and those that have been sitting in the cupboard for months. The useable items should be given away.
- Use this opportunity to clean the cabinets with a damp cloth.
- Rearrange the remaining items in the cupboards neatly. For small pieces, you can implement the use of wire baskets.
- You can buy matching canisters that you can stack neatly for storing items.
- Consider shifting to the open shelving method so you can see what you have at a glance.

6. Decluttering Your Kitchen Countertops

The countertops in the kitchen are the most accessible place to drop your shopping bags and other items once you step into the kitchen. This approach makes them an attractive area for clutter. Clearing clutter on the countertops can be quite easy since the entire space is visible.

Here are some easy steps you can take to complete this process:

- Move the items creating clutter to the floor or your dining table.
- Get a cleaning cloth and soapy water to clean the countertop.
- Inspect the things you have moved from the countertops and separate those that you can donate as well as those that are better off in a different room.
- Move some of the items into various cupboards in the kitchen.
- If your storage space is limited, create zones on the countertop with each zone assigned a selection of similar items.
- Frequently used appliances like a coffee maker or blender can find a spot on the countertop.

- Avoid piling dishes and mail on the countertops.

Your Quick Start Action Step:

Doing the dishes as soon as you are done with your meal or at the end of the day can prevent the pile-up of clutter. Reducing the number of silverware in the kitchen also goes a long way in minimizing clutter. You can quickly get rid of the appliances taking a spot on the countertops if they are not in use.

All these tasks should be included in your daily schedule.

Chapter 7: Bathrooms and Laundry Room

Chapter 7: Bathrooms and Laundry Room

Bathroom

When it comes to bathrooms, decluttering involves removing and organizing the items which take up space in your drawers, shelves, and countertops. It can be surprising to finally find out just how many things you have and how many you have to wade through to find the ones that you need.

Follow these guidelines when deciding to declutter your bathroom:

1. Empty Your Bathroom Drawers and Closet of Everything In Them

When it comes to decluttering, specific experts have recommended going through this process with as many bathrooms as you have at once. This method helps you gain a clear idea of just how much extra stuff you have. For instance, you might have enough bathroom soap to last the year and not be aware of it. Whichever way you aim to do this, it is vital to clear the countertops, clean out the drawers, and thoroughly clean the linen closets in and around your bathrooms.

2. Get Rid of Duplicates

Getting rid of duplicates such as extra brushes, thermometers, hair dyes, body scrubbers, loofahs, and more is a great way to declutter your bathroom. You should get rid of the old items once you purchase new items to replace them. This strategy helps you avoid the build-up of clutter. You should always be aware of things such as extra conditioner, shampoo, body lotion, bar soap, and other skincare products. Make a list of anything that has not been used in six months and get rid of them.

3. Place Similar Items Together

Doing this is a vital step when it comes to organizing and decluttering your bathroom. Make a pile for towels, medicine, cleaning supplies, toiletries, makeup, etc. this helps you to see what you are aiming to remove from your bathroom.

4. Reduce your Counter Clutter

Once you have decided which things you make use of and want to keep, you should put the items that you make use of daily in easy to access locations. Your counters should remain clear and should only contain toothbrushes, hand soap, and toothpaste. If there is not enough storage space, you can make use of a storage box to hold a couple of items. That being said, you should not attempt to turn your counter into a storage space.

5. Cleaning Supplies

You should ensure that everything you keep is something that you find useful. Sponges and brushes that are too old to use should be thrown away. It takes a bit of time to finish a container of cleaner, which is why it is imperative to ensure that you do not have too many surplus items.

Organize your bathroom and ensure it stays that way.

Essential tools for organizing your bathroom are drawer organizers, dividers, small baskets, and boxes. With numerous small items located in the bathroom, it would be time-wasting, not to mention frustrating, if you have to go through every drawer to find the one thing you need. Organizing the clutter in your bathroom is not something that costs money. Search for small containers or plastics located all over the house which can be repurposed into drawer organizers. As with other spaces in the home, you aim to eradicate as many items as possible from your bathroom's countertops. If the items are used daily, they should be neatly organized in a container or placed in a drawer that can be easily accessed.

6. Get Rid of or Donate Any Excess

Most times when decluttering, we discover that there are various containers or bottles of half-empty things in our bathrooms. When we have more than one of the same item, it is best to put them together and get rid of the empty containers or bottles. If you find yourself holding onto an item that has a little bit left, you should give yourself a time limit of a month to use the item. If it not used within that month, it has to be thrown away.

Another item that could be creating bathroom clutter is towels. Most times, we purchase new towels to replace the supposedly worn-out ones. However, we never get rid of the old ones leading us to accumulate more and more of them. Decide what a perfectly suitable number of towels would be for your home. Maybe you can make use of 8 bath towels. It is an excellent number for a family of 3 with two extra towels able to serve any guests or act as spares.

7. Cosmetics

Cosmetics should never be kept for an indefinite period as they are capable of growing bacteria or even expiring. Using them at that point could have adverse consequences. The majority of cosmetics should only be kept for a maximum of a year.

8. Hair Products

There have been periods when I stumbled upon 5-year-old hair gel. One way that we build up clutter in our bathroom is by purchasing a new product to see if it will work for you. After using it, you notice that it doesn't. However, since it would feel incredibly wasteful to throw them away, you keep them only to stumble upon it five years later. You have to get rid of it, especially if you can't remember when you purchased it or when the last time was that someone used it.

9. Prescriptions

It is imperative to throw away any old medicines not being used by anyone. These old prescriptions do nothing but create clutter, and they can also be dangerous if used. Certain pharmacies allow people to turn in old prescriptions.

10. Over the Counter Medication

Things like pain killers, ointments, and creams all come with an expiration date printed on them. These items don't last as long as we think they do. When decluttering, it is not uncommon to come across medication or creams that have expired many years ago. If it is a medication you need to have on standby, you can add it to the shopping list and ensure you replace it.

11. Stock Ups

It is usual for a bathroom to have a stash of items that were purchased due to being on sale. These stock ups have to be decluttered. You have to ensure anything you decide to stock up on is a product that your family uses. You also have to make sure that it will be placed somewhere that makes it visible and available for use before it sits in storage and expires.

12. Skincare Products

These products have to be used every day or at the very least weekly, and if you are not using it as frequently, then you have no need for it. Everyone has face washes, creams, and lotions that were purchased for the sole purpose of making us look youthful, only for them to be relegated to the back of the drawer when we realized it was all a marketing gimmick. You should only store the things that you are using.

13. Hair Accessories

When decluttering your bathroom, you should go through any pins, hair ties, headbands, scarfs, and other hair accessories to ensure that they are still usable. If you discover anything that is broken, you should throw it out. You should fight the urge to put overstretched hair ties back in your drawers.

They should be thrown out once they outlive their usefulness to prevent clutter.

14. Appliances

You might have a non-working electric shaver stored in the bathroom for no reason other than to collect dust. Decluttering gives you the time to realize when you are unable to make good use of a particular appliance, and it would be better if you got rid of it, sold it, or donated it.

15. Travel Samples and Size

You might believe that it is particularly wasteful to get rid of travel-sized items and samples, right? Most times, we keep them somewhere making a mental note to use them on our next trip, but we end up forgetting about them. It is not surprising to find samples older than some of your clothes in a bathroom. The old stuff should be thrown out. If possible, you should donate the unopened items or make use of them. Another way to cut down on waste is not to purchase a new item and make use of the travel-sized item until it is finished.

16. Counter Clutter

You should have a look and make a list of the things that seem to reside on your counter permanently. Ascertain that they deserve to be in that place. We often make a conscientious effort to keep nothing but face wash and hand soap on their bathroom counters because when you decide to add one more thing, it doesn't just end at one more thing. When you have a clear bathroom counter, everyone in that household can understand that there should not be anything left out. It should be put away once it is done being used.

17. Kid Stuff

Bath toys and other age-appropriate stuff should only be kept in the bathroom if the child that owns those things needs them when taking a bath.

Laundry Room

Let's be honest with ourselves for a second: almost every one of us hates having to do laundry. It could be because of how much time it requires, how much it interrupts the day, or just because it is an incredibly mundane task. Trust me. You are not alone. There are quite a lot of people that feel just like this. For most homeowners, the bone of contention isn't quite the act itself; instead, it is because their laundry room is cramped, small, or just plain uninviting. It might appear as an afterthought, but learning how you can organize the place where you do your laundry is a critical step in ensuring the house stays clean. In the majority of homes, a laundry room doubles as a tight space for clothes, piles, towels, and shoes. All that will change because this article is going to show you how you can completely re-vamp your laundry room into one that is organized, welcoming, and functional.

1. Develop Laundry Stations

Do you have a dedicated space where you store your hampers? Is there a dedicated space to not only fold but sort out laundry? Do you often find yourself carrying a big pile of clothes up and down the stairs with nowhere to place them?

This space is where organized laundry spaces or stations earn their keep. Nevertheless, before you can organize, you have to create a system that enables you and everyone else in the household to maintain that room's clutter-free, clean, and spacious state.

You should use the following variables as guidelines when creating a functional laundry station:

2. Counter Space

The whole point of organizing is to make your life simpler. One way of doing that is to have sufficient access to folding tables or counter space. When you have available counter space, you are more inclined to fold, hang, and put your clothes away once they are taken out of the dryer or washer.

3. Drying Rack

It does not matter if you prefer to dry your clothes on a drying rack or hangers; you must make at least one of these spaces available. You can also make use of tension rods to dry your clothes if you are space conscious.

4. Laundry Baskets

Ensure you have a laundry basket or hamper situated in your laundry room. This approach helps you to unload and load your items quickly while doing laundry. Generally, these can be placed either in a closet nearby or underneath your counters.

5. Ironing Board

Rather than storing wrinkled clothes away and then ironing them right before you have to wear them, you should have an ironing board situated in the laundry room. This action helps you unwrinkle your outfits faster. Doing this not only saves you time and hassle but also saves space in the long-term.

6. Make the Most of the Space You Already Have

A laundry room is supposed to be solely for washing, drying, and ironing our clothes, however, it ends up serving as a multipurpose room. It stores our coats, towels, shoes, pet supplies, backpacks, and more. A great way to organize all of these items is to make use of vertical storage. Vertical storage enables you to make the most of your available space while keeping it uncluttered.

Make use of every bit of space the laundry room has by using shelves, wall units, and hanging baskets. See below for more details on how to maximize the use of your laundry room:

Make use of wall space

Certain people see the laundry room as an entry point into the house, which is why it is imperative to have dedicated areas for your shoes, irrespective of the season. DIY shoe racks can be a way to stop anyone from tracking in dirt and grass through the house. These racks are easy to set up and also cost-effective. They can be manufactured from floating shelves, tension rods, or PVC pipes. They can also be stored on a solid wall.

You can invest in hooks, baskets, and shelves

They are simple solutions that make it seamless for you to store your items while also preventing the build-up of clutter. Dryer sheets and laundry detergents can be placed in wire racks or shelving above the dryer and washer. Jackets, backpacks, hats, and accessories can be stored on hooks placed on the wall.

Smaller things can be placed inside decorative baskets. This step ensures the floor space remains open and clean.

A great way to maximize your space is to consider any hidden storage that might not be so apparent. You might consider hanging items over the door. The laundry room door is not just for keeping the noise down. Its back can become a beautiful place to store an ironing board until it is required. This way of storing items is even made more straightforward thanks to over the door storage organizers which enable you to keep your things out of view.

Select the correct laundry storage solution

Learning the proper way to organize a laundry room is not just about cleaning and then moving things around. Once you figure out how you can make the most out of your space and also create the required number of laundry stations, you have to make sure that you have the storage containers capable of handling your laundry supplies.

Consider purchasing the following containers to have the best solution for your laundry room storage:

Closed containers are useful to help hide away your laundry essentials. They also ensure the room looks much more organized. Open containers can be used to store bleach bottles and laundry detergent boxes.

Canvas containers or lined baskets can be used to clean up after spills.

Small items such as stain sticks, pocket change, lone socks, and laundry markers can be stored using small boxes. You should ensure that these containers can easily be accessed when you are in your laundry room. This effort not only helps to keep your dedicated spaces organized, but it also hides the laundry essentials from guests when they come over.

Consider purchasing appliances that help to save space

It is true, dryers and washers tend to take up a lot of space; however, that does not mean we should give up and let them take over the laundry room. This tip is a great idea to go with if you are in the market for a new dryer or washer. It is also great if you are looking to downsize to a smaller yet more efficient appliance. You should always remember that less can be more. Using a smaller dryer or washer could give you more space to work within your laundry room and your home at large. It could also create an area that is much more functional for your household.

There are numerous benefits to purchasing a washer and dryer combo appliance:

- You can fit your smaller stacked devices into smaller spaces such as closets, apartments, or studios.
- Smaller dryers and washers tend to be equipped with bottom drawers which provide additional hidden storage.
- Dryers and washers that save space do more than just that. They are particularly efficient, which helps to save on the utility bills as well as reduce your carbon footprint, and save the environment.

Your Quick Start Action Step:

Clearing out expired medications in the bathroom and empty containers of soap and other items can free up a lot of space.

A laundry basket in the laundry room is also a tremendous help to properly store your laundry. You can use this in limiting clutter on the floors.

Chapter 8: Closets

Chapter 8: Closets

The closet is a vital storage space in the home in which you can keep your clothes, shoes, and other items out of sight. Since the items inside are not visible, it is easy to overlook the clutter you create inside the closet.

When decluttering, you should try to simplify the process by decluttering based on the type of clothing you have in the closet. To this end, you need to categorize the objects into boots, denim, dresses, shoes, coats, and so on. You should understand that it is much simpler to identify the dresses that you don't need anymore when you are looking at all the dresses you own rather than a mix of your dresses and jeans collection.

How to Declutter Your closets

1. Take Out the Items in the Closet

    This is a step that simplifies your decluttering process. As soon as you take out the objects filling up the closet, you can identify those that are in the wrong storage space. Out of the pile of clothes and other objects from the cabinet, these identified items should be screened out.

Clearing out the closet provides the opportunity to clean the interior of the cabinets properly.

2. Discard Some Items

Regardless of the number of clothes or shoes you own, there will only be a few of these that you wear most of the time. This tip gives you room to rid your closets of most of the clothes and shoes that you store in them. If you are finding it difficult to reach a decision, answering these questions can help:

- Did you wear it on any day during the last six months?
- Is the item faded, stained, or torn?
- Is it still an excellent fit?

Clothing articles you need to get rid of are easily identifiable through the answers you give to these questions.

3. Move Your Seasonal Clothes

Seasonal clothes take up a reasonable amount of space in the closet but don't get used often. You can move seasonal clothes and shoes into a storage box or bin to create space in the closet. The bin can be kept under the bed or in a storage room until the contents are required.

4. Organize the Closet from the Bottom and Move Towards the Top

When rearranging the objects back into the closet, you should start arranging from the bottom of the closet and work your way to the objects that will be at the top. The simple reason for this is to prevent interference from hanging clothes as you try to put the closet in order.

5. Learn to Make Use of Vertical Spaces

Adding a new closet for more storage is usually not an option. Instead, you can make the most of what's already in place. The back of the closet door, top of the shelf, and wall offer excellent storage opportunities if adequately utilized. You can hang your scarves, robes, jewelry, and other items on hooks. Besides, rather than an entire closet, you can add a shelf at the top for objects that you need on special occasions.

6. Incorporate the Use of Bins, Robe Hooks, or Baskets

The purpose of the bins, baskets, or robe hooks is to provide additional storage. The clothing items that go into these storage spaces are those that you can wear at least twice before you need to wash. Creating special storage for these clothes prevents wrinkling, separates them from the clean clothes in the closet, and reduces closet clutter.

Your Quick Start Action Step:

Folding clothes in a neat stack is an excellent way to minimize clutter in your closets. You should also hang clothes by their length to make them easy to access and to give a clear view of what you have in the closet.

Try to separate clothing that can move to a different storage space such as coats and hats.

Chapter 9:
Storage Room

Chapter 9: Storage Room

A storage room is usually one of the most challenging places to declutter in the home. It is the room where we stuff all the various items that we don't plan on using anytime soon, those that have lost their value, those with sentimental value, and those that we are unsure of dealing with. The things you accumulate in this room, as well as the various boxes present, make it overwhelming anytime you decide to declutter your storage room.

The overwhelming feeling that sweeps you shows the effect of turning your storage room into a dump for anything you are indecisive on. The amount of clutter in this room can sometimes be worth years of your life. Another issue with this space is that, since it is out of sight, it is usually out of mind.

There are various reasons why decluttering the storage space in your home is crucial. These are some of the reasons you should consider:

It Lifts a Burden Off Your Shoulders

The problem with clutter is that it often affects you mentally. The idea that you don't think about clutter if you don't see it doesn't necessarily mean that you are free from the problems the clutter creates. A storage space that is packed full prevents you from moving items from other areas of the home into the storage room.

Since there is no other storage space available, clutter steadily builds up inside the home. The physical clutter that forms also creates a mental clutter anytime you start considering how many possessions you have accumulated and the need to rid your house of clutter. Mental clutter can also develop anytime you have to think of where you may have kept an item.

You Understand That More Storage Space is Not the Solution You Require

Your desire for more storage space will increase every time you consider the amount of clutter in your home. You easily overlook the fact that it is possible to fill up as many storage spaces as possible without getting rid of clutter.

Decluttering helps you find the things you don't like or need so you can eliminate them from the home to create room for those that are required. After the decluttering process, it is easy to learn that if you limit your possessions to those things that you need, you will have enough storage space in the home to hold the items.

This effort prevents additional expenses you can incur due to renovations or moving to a bigger house.

Steps to Take in Decluttering Your Storage Room

1. Perform a Quick Surface Decluttering

Surface decluttering doesn't require as much time and effort as deep purge decluttering. In this case, you are merely looking for the items lying around the storage room that you can throw in the trash without giving it a second thought. These include those that are broken and those without any value, both sentimental and monetary value.

If you are feeling overwhelmed by the amount of clutter in the storage space, this is a great way to start. It is much better if you focus on starting with the small items during this step. As soon as you clear out these small items, you can then work your way up through the larger pieces. Broken sports equipment and furniture can go for repairs and then to a donation center, or you can sell them.

The larger the size of the item you remove, the more space you create and the easier it becomes to work in the room.

2. Create Clutter Piles to Classify Items with Similar Functions

Your storage room will contain lots of items with different functions and uses. Amid these items, you are sure to find several items offering similar features. These are items you separate into one pile.

The reason for creating a pile is to find out which items you need to discard based on their number. If you find out you have several cartons filled with dishes you received as gifts or extras from a set, you should donate the excess to people that will appreciate them more. No matter the number of individuals living in your home, you should only require dishes that can cater for two day's worth of meals. Piling up unwashed dishes for more than two days in itself is an unhealthy habit.

All your duplicate items should be given out, including your extra hammers, bags, pans, and so on. Upon classification of these items, you will also find those that don't match your contemporary lifestyle. Let go of these items. You may find your hiking backpacks and boots lying around, but if you have no intention of taking a hike for a long time, you can donate or sell these items.

3. Guide Your Decisions Using Decluttering Questions

The major questions that help with the decluttering process are as follows:

- Do I love this item?
- When was the last time I used this item?
- Is there a reason for having more than one of these items?

These are just some basic questions that can be of immense help while decluttering. Some individuals often fail to understand that once an item has been in the storage room for a few months without the need to use it, it is time to dispose of it. This failure makes the decluttering process difficult.

If you develop a form of discipline while decluttering, you can stick to making the right decisions based on the answers you give to the above questions concerning an object. Some items are not worth the time it takes to move them into storage or the storage space they take up.

4. Ruthlessness is a Crucial Skill for Decluttering

Sentiments will get in the way of decluttering if you fail to develop a ruthless side. Considering the cost of purchasing a particular object can prevent you from throwing it out despite it being useless. Being ruthless makes all these irrelevant.

If you decide that all items that are of no use both now and in the future must be eliminated from the home, ruthlessness allows you to follow this decision through until the end. When decluttering some rooms in the house, you have some items that go into the "maybe box'." These are items that usually fill up the storage space.

This approach is why you no longer have room for indecision when you get to decluttering your storage space. Check the different labels on the boxes. If some have been in the storage space for over six months, or over a year for seasonal items, it is time to dispose of the items in the box.

If you think the need for an item will still crop up in the future, you should consider ridding the home of those that can be purchased at a very affordable price and within a 20-minute time duration. You should also find those that you can rent when you need them to work.

5. Items With Sentimental Value

These are objects that you love, those you received from a loved one who has passed away or those that trigger a particular memory.

Sentimental items can be a challenge to declutter and to address this issue. There will be an in-depth discussion in a later chapter.

6. Keep Your Possessions in Check by Imposing Space Restrictions

Categorizing items has a lot of benefits when you decide to declutter. The benefits that this action offers include a quick look at how many items you have in a particular category and the ease of organizing similar items in a specific location.

When you decide to organize similar items in a specific location, it provides the opportunity to limit the amount of space you allocate to these items. Your storage space is going to be split into several sections to cover all the things you intend to keep.

By allocating space, it becomes easy to determine when you are accumulating more of a particular category without making use of the items you already have. If you are disciplined in your approach, you will see to it that these items do not extend past the allocated space by getting rid of some things.

The limit you impose on each category depends on the size of the storage room.

7. Don't Rush the Process

Once you start rushing the decluttering process, you end up letting objects without value back into the home. It is a much better option to perform the decluttering process over a few days rather than rushing it with unsatisfactory results.

Make sure that each item you take out of the storage space is carefully considered before gaining access back inside.

8. Make Sure You Properly Arrange the Storage Space After decluttering

Now you have completed the process of decluttering; the next step is to make sure that you put the storage space in order. By carefully organizing the storage space, you can further reduce the visual clutter that is caused by disorganization.

As mentioned earlier, create sections for each category of items in the storage space. You can then add a label to indicate the category that occupies a particular area. Your organization of the space should ensure that access to items in the storage space is effortless. This outcome will reduce your stress anytime you have to come to search for something.

Your Quick Start Action Step:

If you want to see tangible results in large areas like your storage spaces, dedicate specific days to check the maybe boxes. These are boxes of items you are unsure of their fate. Getting rid of those that have been there for over six months without being touched can free up space in the storage.

Create a reminder by including the date on which it will be exactly six months after taking a maybe box to your storage room.

You can also get rid of old equipment and electronics on this date.

Chapter 10: Entryways, Mudrooms, and Foyers

Chapter 10: Entryways, Mudrooms, and Foyers

The entryway, mudroom, or foyer is a part of the house whose primary purpose is to store objects that we take out daily and to connect the outside of the house to the inside. The entryway is quite easy to identify with its linoleum flooring and the inclusion of a coat closet.

A mudroom is quite similar to the entryway except it doesn't appear in all homes. This area makes it more of a secondary, less important entryway. Nonetheless, it is quite useful in the storage of shoes, wet clothing, outerwear, and footwear to ensure the cleanliness of the home's interior.

Depending on the design of the house, the entryway can vary from a very spacious one to a minimal space. Due to the high traffic through this area of the home, it must remain clutter-free. Decorations are of minor concern in the entryway.

The other purpose that makes the entryway an essential part of the home is that it offers storage spaces. These are spaces where visitors and members of the family can keep their stuff for the duration they will be inside and easily pick it up when it is time to leave.

There are various things you want your entryway or mudroom to hold. These are the things that visitors and family members frequently carry into the home on their way in. Some of the items you should create space for in the entryway include the following:

- Different types of bags such as the briefcases, school bags, purses, backpacks, and gym bags
- Jackets and coats
- Your mail
- Shoes
- Umbrellas, hats, scarves, gloves and other weather-related clothing or accessories
- Electronics, coins, keys, cellphones, and other items in the pockets of an individual

There are various reasons why you should consider having a clutter-free entryway in the home. It makes it easy to find your essential possessions as you head out for the day. However, that isn't the only reason you should keep this area clutter-free. Read on to the next section to find out more.

Why it is Important to Declutter Your Entryway

There are some simple reasons why you should put in extra effort to declutter this space in the home. Some of these essential reasons include:

To Prevent Frustration

When the entryway is cluttered, it becomes challenging to find the items you need to get to work. It becomes annoying if you have to search through numerous things for your essential possessions like shoes, a briefcase, or umbrella under a pile of clutter. Your frustration builds up due to the unnecessary items you keep seeing as you continue your search.

To Avoid Embarrassment

Neighbors and friends are guests that you will need to entertain sooner or later. The entryway is the first place that these guests enter when visiting your home. The first impression that guests get out of a cluttered entryway lowers their expectations for your home. It is an embarrassing situation to have your friends see your house full of clutter.

You Waste Less Time

Your morning routine might involve getting dressed in your room and then moving to the entryway to complete your preparation for work. This preparation will include taking out your shoes, outerwear, and bag. If there is lots of clutter covering the area, it becomes difficult to take what you need.

You waste more time searching for these items, and you often leave home late. Removing clutter in this area saves you time when preparing for work.

Steps to Take in Decluttering

1. Discard Non-essential Items

Typical clutter that takes space in the entryway and mudroom includes broken umbrellas, work boots with soles peeled off, old coats no longer in use, and other damaged items. Take time to remove these items that create clutter in the entryway.

2. Place a Trash Bin Close By

If there is a trash bin close to the entryway, it makes it easier to dispose of your waste when stepping into the house or heading out. This placement can be useful if you want to immediately get rid of junk mail before it makes its way into the home to create paper clutter.

3. Restrict the Items That Should Be in This Space

To ensure that you minimize clutter in the entryway or the mudroom, it is vital you make a home rule to restrict the items that are stored here. This guideline may involve limiting the number of shoes per individual, separating objects that are better off in another storage space or controlling the number of hats or coats you hang by the door. By imposing this restriction, you can prevent members of your family from creating a mess anytime they come in.

4. Make Use of Baskets

Cane or wicker baskets not only offer great aesthetics, but they are also an excellent form of storage. You can decide on the number of baskets that should be in the entryway or mudroom depending on the needs of your home. Use the baskets in sorting and organizing any item that will stay in the entryway or mudroom.

5. Store Objects on the Wall

Decluttering is about making sure there is a storage space for different items. To create more storage space in your entryway, look towards the wall to properly utilize the vertical space available. You can make use of labeled tags or fancy hooks to store umbrellas, bags, and coats with ease. This implementation makes them easily accessible when making your way out of the house.

6. Install Small Cupboards

Cabinets or cupboards in the entryway can be useful if they have several drawers installed. They occupy minimal entryway space but offer a reasonable amount of storage. The idea of selecting a small cupboard is to provide a restriction on the number of items that make their way into the cabinets. To make more productive use of the cupboard, each drawer can have a label to indicate the objects that go into a specific drawer.

Your Quick Start Action Step:

Broken umbrellas, shoes caked in mud, and old work boots are items that can easily be discarded from this area. If you don't have any, you can install hooks on the wall to make room for coats and hats.

Chapter 11:
Home Office

Chapter 11: Home Office

The home office is a room where you get work done. This area may be used for your business, a project, or any task you take home from the office. It is the one room where you can improve your productivity and focus.

It is common to find clutter in this room, and there are simple steps you can take to declutter.

Decluttering the Home Office

1. Don't Mix Business and Pleasure

Having a section of your home double as your office isn't a bad idea. But you've got to keep it organized. Taking off anything that does not relate to your work is a great way to decongest the desk and clear off all items not suitably placed. You pay deductibles to the Internal Revenue Service if the home office is used exclusively for business purposes. However, you can avoid this deductible if you try to create another role for the office, maybe by also using it as a guest room. But, you should separate your business room from your leisure room by attending to your guests or working on your crafts in a different location.

2. Go Through Paper Items

Usually, the office is home to different clutter, including relevant documents and trash. It is there you find piles of bills, documents, receipts, invoices, and other pieces of paper. The task of ensuring a less muddled office becomes easier once you start clearing off the paper. Doing this begins with sorting the different pieces of paper into sections in order of importance. We can sort them into Files, To-do, and Junk. In that way, you can do your cabinet filing properly, shred, and trash the junk pile. The To-do pile can remain in a basket next to your desk to remind yourself of the files that need urgent attention.

Let us examine some of the tips to help you remove clutter from your home office:

- Scan all relevant documents, invoices, and receipts. Make a digital record of the papers.

- Try to shred all the paper you won't need anymore.
- Store older files in a plastic bin and keep them away from the office space. You can store them in the basement, garage, or you create a space for them, but let it be outside the office.
- Set aside a particular space for vital mail, paper, or documents that need urgent attention.
- Ensure circular files are appropriately filed when you're doing your filing paperwork.

3. Clear Off Your Desk

The desk is not a storeroom, so try as much as possible to take away all papers and documents that should be in the cabinet or drawers. Only keep items that you use frequently or that need urgent action on the desk. Never allow any food or oil close to the desk, computer, table lamp, or other desk essentials. Make optimal use of the office drawers. You can keep a few embellishments on the desk, but don't add so many you reduce the desk's functionality.

4. Clean Out and Organize Drawers

Take regular cleaning of the drawers and office cabinets seriously. The drawers shouldn't look like piles of junk when you open them. There are three simple steps you can take to take care of your office supplies:

5. Empty the Office Drawers

The first action is to take everything out of the drawers. Just as the desk is not meant for unimportant and non-urgent items and documents, the drawers are also not meant to keep papers that will not be needed for over a year. Take away documents that you have not used for (six) months. If there is a necessity to keep these files in the office, you can buy small boxes or containers to keep them. Arrange files in such a way that like-items stay near each other. This step will help you avoid a free-floating of objects in the drawers.

6. Pruning Files

While it is often recommended that you

keep files and papers for some time before you discard them, it is also imperative to section these files to avoid disorganized drawers. Take time at least once every six months to check these files. Put them into sections of current files, archival files, and obsolete files. Move the archival files to a box that you have clearly labeled. Get rid of the old files.

7. Invest in a Shredder

Do not discard papers, documents, and files carelessly. Be careful with paper that carries your name, signature, and personal or official identity, including bank account, legal agreement, etc. Shredding them before discarding them will help you reduce the risk of identity theft. Purchase some shredders and a wastebasket and put them within reach to be sure that your documents are adequately shredded and disposed of.

8. Tame Your Cords

The crisp, fantastic look you want for your home office desk can be achieved only if you ensure that you wrangle in your cords. Keep the essential in the home office. Try to go online and search for a couple of cord management products that are used to tie up and tame cords. Below are a few of cord hacks you can use:

- Try to label cords with tape. With this, it becomes easier to tell what cable goes with each device.
- Hold cords that are co unplugged up on your desk with binder clips.
- Use twist-ties or rubber bands to tie up excess cables.

9. Create a Printing Station

Never cluster old and in-use printers in one place. Designate a space in the office for your printer and printer supplies. Wireless printers don't need to stay on the desk. Place them in a cabinet or create a space for them in the office.

10. Create a Mail Station

Mail is the most likely paper to come into the office, and you will need to stay in control to keep it from accumulating. Try to create a mail station by making a folder for incoming and outgoing mail. Also, make a folder for every family member. As soon as the mail comes in, quickly file it in the mail station.

11. Use Office Organizers for Clutter Control

Partition office supplies into various sections. You can do this by organizing items of similar purpose in the same place while 'unlike' items are placed separately. You can keep stationery together and papers in another section. Again, try to store all mail supplies in one drawer, and so on. In this way, you won't have the stress of ransacking the entire box or cabinet of files while searching for one file, thus ending up disorganizing the whole place. Meanwhile, if your storage and space are limited, try to use the vertical arrangement method.

Installing shelves on the wall is a great idea that will help create enough space for your items and documents. Shelving will also give you room to arrange your files, books, work manuals, and materials in a place you can easily have access to them. It also helps you with hanging filing systems and lots more. Never leave the shelves hanging without support. To achieve a perfect result, try to stage shelves with pretty office organizers such as hanging wire baskets, bins, drawers, boxes, etc. Floating shelves are not suitable for large rooms, so only use them in relatively small rooms. The reason for this is that floating shelves don't demand corbels or brackets for their installation. Try to reduce the clutter on your home office desk to 20% covered or less. Use a tall armoire in your office as it gives a ton of additional storage opportunities where you can stash your wireless printer. Never dump junk items on your desk.

Your Quick Start Action Step:

Take time every day to shred any junk mail or document with information that shouldn't be exposed. If you don't have a shredder, invest in one as soon as you can. Clear your desk of any clutter as soon as you are through with work for the day.

Chapter 12: Basement and Attic

Chapter 12: Basement and Attic

The attic and basement are two storage spaces that are found in the home. While the basement is usually below the ground floor in the house, you can expect to see the attic directly below the roof. The use of attics and basements as storage areas is usually due to the difficulty accessing these areas as well as the lack of comfort due to their design. Despite these issues, you can still find some of these spaces converted into a room or office in several homes.

As storage spaces, the attic and basement are places where you load items you are sure you won't need for a long time, those that you keep for sentimental value, outdated products, and things that you haven't decided what to do with. The selections of items that go into these spaces usually create clutter in the rooms. Your inability to discard these items means you keep stuffing these items until you run out of space.

When it is time to declutter these storage spaces, don't kid yourself into thinking you can complete the decluttering in a few hours. You need to dedicate a few days to decluttering an attic or basement.

The strategy you apply in this room is the divide and conquer strategy. By separating the room into zones, you can choose a zone to focus on first before moving on to the next area. This strategy eases your workload and makes the process less overwhelming.

Steps to Declutter Your Basement or Attic

1. Split your Attic or Basement into Various Segments

First, segment attic and basement organization into six easy steps. With this, you can declutter your basement without feeling stressed out.

To make work in your basement easy, you should take it one section at a time. Get started by working on a stack of boxes, kid's toys, and clothes that are no longer in use, periodic decorations and shelves.

While working in a particular segment, take time to complete that segment before moving on to another. If you are focusing on bins, ensure that all bins are emptied. If shelves are what you want to focus on first, ensure they are cleared completely. It will be very distracting to start working on another segment when you are not done with the previous section.

2. Everything Should Be Sorted Into Bins

Since you are focused on an area in your basement that is used in storing stuff, it is okay to take out one bin and concentrate your attention there to either dispose of the items you come across or holding on to them. While at this, if you come across anything that you think can be fixed without you having to spend too much, it is okay to have a different pile for such items. To make sure that you end up fixing such things, it is vital that you set a deadline. If the deadline comes and goes before you fix them, you should go ahead and dispose of them.

3. Take the Items You Intend to Dispose of Out of the House

Before separating the items that you intend to keep, you should take everything that you want to dispose of out of your house. Once outside ensure that they are all kept in the trash bin. If you do not intend to throw them away but plan to donate them, you should move them straight into the vehicle that you will use to move them away from your house. If you are not donating them immediately, it is okay to keep them in your garage for a while.

4. Keep Items That Are Alike in One Piece

The same tips that can help you organize your bathroom can be applied when getting your basement decluttered. Keeping similar items in one pace will make it very easy for you to have access to them whenever you need them. Are you in possession of ornaments that can be used to decorate trees? If yes, you should then keep decorations of similar colors together. By doing this, when next you want to decorate a tree, there will be no need to get out all the boxes with ornaments, you can pick the color you want.

5. Ensure Bins and Boxes Are Labeled

While putting already sorted out items back into bins and boxes, you must label all the things you are putting into the boxes. If you don't want to write on the bin, it is okay to have a list of the contents of the container written on a piece of paper and then paste it on the bin. This way, you can know the contents without opening it. Another way to do this is to make use of a label maker to put removable but semi-permanent labels on the bin. It is easier to have an idea of what is inside if you make use of clear bins.

Your Quick Start Action Step:

The quick action step here is similar to your other storage spaces. Take out old junk that is not going to be needed anytime soon.

Chapter 13: Books and Paper Documents

Chapter 13: Books and Paper Documents

Books and paper documents easily create clutter in the home. Paper tends to scatter around due to their lightweight and possibly clutter the house. The zeal to gather information and learn more about a topic make books a necessity in the home. Unfortunately, having a lot of books could also lead to clutter.

These books and paper documents need to be decluttered regularly. Otherwise, they would quickly gather in the home if you're not careful.

Getting Books and Paper Documents Decluttered

1. Arrange Your Books or Documents in Different Categories

To successfully declutter your books and other paper documents, it is essential you know exactly what you have. You can achieve this by bringing all these items out of their hiding spots and then placing them in front of you. You can then separate them into different categories.

Categorizing the books and paper documents is an essential step for those that consider themselves book lovers. However, the number of books you have will be impossible to declutter in one sitting. The categories you can split these items into include:

- Magazines

- Visual books (art books, coffee table books, etc.)

- General books (books you read for fun)

- Children's books

- Practical books (reference books, cookbooks, etc.)

2. Identify the Books That Get Your Heart Racing

To make the process very useful, it is best to treat all your books as if you intend to dispose of all of them. Give each book an equal chance of being kept by looking through all of them and then coming up with a decision on the books that you intend to continue reading.

While trying to sort out books, Marie Kondo has made it known to her students that it is best they do not go on to read these books while they are still being handled and thinking of the books to keep. The reason is that going this route will end up making the entire process never-ending. It will also make it a lot more challenging to choose which books should be kept and which books should be disposed of.

What if you suddenly think to yourself, "I may like to reread it another time."

One major challenge many people face when disposing of books is the thought that a day will come when they would like to read the same book over again. This mindset makes it difficult to discard the books that you should dispose of.

To people facing the challenge of wanting to read a book sometime later, it is possible you never really want to read the book. You rarely find people that pick up books that have been on the shelf for a period and go through them or read them a second time if they have read them before. And due to this, there is nothing wrong in disposing of a book you intend to read later.

It is a better option to read a book the first time you come across it as that is the best time to do so. If you are unable to read a book the first time you get ahold of it, the chance that you would read it another time is very slim.

Nothing is absolute, and some people are exceptions to this statement.

Sometimes, you will notice that you are longing for a book that you have recently donated. In this case, a more suitable option is to look for an electronic copy of the book. The information is usually the same, although some people say they prefer reading the physical copy of a book.

3. Those That Don't Get Your Heart Racing Should be Discarded

There are certain books you read that get your heart racing and make you ponder what will happen next. Then there are those that you struggle to get to the end. There is a vast difference between these books. Those that get your heart racing are the books you are likely to read again. For the second group, you would be doing yourself a favor by disposing of them.

There are different ways to dispose of books. You can try giving them to a church or the neighborhood library. The Amazon FBA program offers an opportunity for individuals to sell off their books with ease. Also, you often experience a form of pleasure anytime you dispose of some of your books to eliminate clutter and create space.

4. Arrange the Leftover Books Properly

As soon as we have taken out all the books that we were not excited about, the next step is to reorganize those that are left in the home. Since you already separated them based on categories, you should do the same when organizing them back onto the shelves. Avoid stacking the books when arranging as this makes it easier for them to fall off.

If you have excess space, then mixing between stacking and standing the books can help close up the spaces between books to prevent them from falling off. Only in situations like this should you consider stacking books.

Questions to Ask to Make Decluttering Easier

Have I gone through the book? Is it one I would love to sit down to read another time?

Do you have a book that you have already read once and do not have any plans to reread it? If yes, then there is no need to keep the book as it is now of no purpose on your shelf. More often than not, novels fall into this group. The only exceptions are when these novels contain some life-transforming stories that you might want to go through a couple more times.

Do you have a book that you are yet to go through? Do you have any plans to read it tomorrow or the day after? If going through this book is not something you are excited about; it is best to give it up. There are lots of books in the world, and you will only have the opportunity to read a handful of these books throughout your life. So, if you have a book you think you will not read, you should not let it occupy space.

Do you use the book frequently?

If you have to always refer to a book, you should not dispose of it. It still meets a pressing need and should be kept.

Is it an extra copy?

Having multiple copies of the same book in your home library might seem funny. But it is possible. You might not believe you have duplicates in your library until you double check, such as finding a paperback version before realizing that you also have a hardcover version of the same book.

Are you sentimental about the book?

You should not hold on to a book out of sentiment. A lot of times, we keep books that we do not need because they came as gifts. If you have a book that is of no use, you should ask yourself if you would keep such a book if it were not a gift.

What are the reasons I am keeping this book?

This is a question you should ask yourself. A lot of people keep their old books for the appearance it gives the home. The truth is even if you dispose of those unwanted books, your home will still look good and even better space-wise.

Is the book available at the library?

Libraries contain a lot more books than you have in your home. If you can get a book at the library, it is okay to let it go.

Is the magazine or book outdated?

Trying to keep books that don't hold relevant information can be quite straightforward to deal with. This scenario can include keeping old travel guides, textbooks, and magazines. A lot of people have unintentionally continued holding on to magazines that promoted trends that are now outdated. This is in addition to keeping travel guides that advertise places that no one would want to visit anymore. The truth remains that a lot of the fantastic restaurants that you would have loved to visit about three decades ago are no longer what they used to be. So, one question you have to ask yourself is, "Are the many magazines I have in my possession still important? Can their contents still be beneficial to me?" If your answer is no, then, you do not need them.

Will these books be important to someone else?

Realizing that others would benefit greatly from a book that you are still holding on to will make it easier to dispose of. It is a lot better to release a book that you are sure will only make your shelf look better if others benefit significantly from it.

Your Quick Start Action Step:

Simply returning books to shelves and arranging magazines back into the magazine racks can quickly remove clutter from a space. Add it to your schedule to organize books and documents.

Chapter 14: Garage

Chapter 14: Garage

The garage used to be nothing more than a space for parking cars, keeping your motorcycles, and storing bicycles. As years roll by, this area of the home has become very important in the lives of many individuals.

There are lots of reasons why the garage remains a crucial space in most homes. For most men, they get the opportunity to flex their creativity when they spend time in their garage. It is from this space that furniture and DIY projects come to life. It is how they create memories.

Besides creating personal memories, it is also a great place to create memories with the kids. You get to bond as you both struggle to paint a cupboard, fix a bicycle tire, build a new dog house, and many more activities.

In addition to the fun activities you can engage in, the garage also offers room for anything that needs to be stored. Tools, a workbench, bicycle racks, lawnmowers, and many more are easily accessible when stored in this space. You can create a mess without considering the implications.

The lack of implications is usually what leads to clutter in the garage. Flexing your creativity gives room for incomplete projects to make a home in the garage. The opportunity to store anything in the garage also gives you the freedom to leave items from ten years ago laying around.

To address the clutter in the garage, the divide and conquer strategy is most effective. You don't have the luxury of selecting what items move to better storage since this is usually where you move things you are indecisive about. The decluttering process involves being ruthless in letting go of useless items.

Steps to Declutter the Garage

The steps you take to declutter should involve paying attention to specific groups of similar items that commonly cause garage clutter. In this section, the steps given relate to many of the everyday objects you find in the garage.

1. Suspend Bicycles on the Wall or Racks

The garage offers great storage space for

bicycles in the home. You must create a room to store them properly. Whatever storage space you create for storing bikes should not impede traffic through the garage.

You can purchase a bicycle rack at a closet accessory store or bicycle shop. Make sure you get one that is sturdy and durable. Depending on the design you select, you can also get baskets or shelves for keeping water bottles, gloves, helmets, and other biking gear. Use screws in fastening the bicycle gear to a wall in the garage.

Another option is to visit a hardware store to buy clips that you can use in suspending the bicycles from the wall.

2. Store Your Athletic Gear Properly

Depending on the sports gear you want to store, you can purchase shelves or racks specially designed to suit your needs. Walk into any closet accessories shop or home center to find shelves that meet your specifications.

You can also put your creativity to work by

designing a storage device for sports equipment at a much cheaper cost. The various sports equipment that should go into the shelves, racks, or DIY storage devices include soccer balls, golf clubs, baseball bats, skis, tennis rackets, and in-line skates.

For your protective gear, you can install hooks or shelves close to the garage entrance so that they are easy easily accessible and visible to anyone that needs them.

3. Purchase Wheeled Storage

These are for sports gear and camping equipment that you will be loading into your car frequently. Instead of letting them occupy space close to the vehicle, put them in wheeled storage that is easy to move around. Doing so makes it suitable for easing the stress of loading and unloading items.

4. Purchase a Fold-down Table

Your repair activities will be challenging unless you have a table to use. The garage is a great place to perform these repairs and also store the table. You must get a table that you can fold to ensure that traffic space in the garage remains free since it can align vertically with the wall.

You can open the table and lock it in place horizontally anytime you need it for work.

5. Discard Old Catalogs, Magazines, and Newspapers

Once any of these items find its way into the garage, it means it is no longer of use to anyone in the home. You should dispose of these items to rid your garage of the clutter they create. If this is a challenge, then start by keeping special editions while disposing of the rest.

6. You Don't Need Those Old Electronics

The garage is an excellent place to store things you want to keep out of sight. These include your old electronics like your fax machine, computers, and printers. If these items are far behind what current technology offers, then you should decide to let go of these items. Donating these items may not be easy, but you are sure to find a recycling program that will accept these items.

7. Tools

The tools you keep in the garage are often a considerable part of the clutter in this storage space. The first set of tools you should go after are those that are broken. If it has been sitting on the shelf for over six months without getting repaired, then you don't need it anymore. Throw these tools out of the home.

You should also check for tools that serve as duplicates and dispose of the excess. You may purchase different toolsets and find specific items that you already own. Keeping five hammers or band hack saws isn't an excellent idea for creating a clutter-free garage.

8. Paint Cans

The reason why you probably have a lot of paint cans in your garage is due to the long shelf life of the contents. Paint can stay good for as long as ten years if you don't open the containers while those that have been used at one point can still last as long as five years. It is common for individuals to decide to keep the leftover paint from a home improvement project.

Depending on how long the paint cans have been in your garage, it may finally be time to let them go. Drop the cans at a waste disposal close by or find out programs concerning paint recycling near you.

9. Leftover Materials

Paint cans are just a part of the leftover clutter from a home improvement project that you are holding on to. There are other materials like paint trays and brushes as well as DIY tools that you are keeping around. Unless there is an upcoming project you have in mind, you should dispose of these items. You are likely going to purchase new tools before remembering you have some old tools when planning for another project anyway.

10. Old Forms of Entertainment

DVDs, CDs, and Online Streaming are just

some of the current options available for your entertainment. Besides these options, there was a time when your home entertainment was dependent on cassette tapes, VHS tapes, a VCR, and tape players. Well, that time is past, and no one would enjoy going through the trouble of flipping to the B-Side to see the end of a movie.

If these tapes are collections of old albums or movies, you can start searching for them in digital formats. As soon as you get the digital formats, you can start getting rid of the physical copies.

11. Décor

Many forms of home décor make up garage clutter. It may merely be some holiday decorations that are no longer in vogue. Others may be an old chair that needs the fabric changed. If you have forgotten about these items, then you can start thinking of how to push them out of the house finally. Thrift stores can help with this or take them to a donation center.

Your Quick Start Action Step:

Remove all the work tools laying around, arrange them in a toolbox, or hang them on hooks on the wall. Simply putting bicycles on their racks and clearing them off the pathway can make the garage seem clutter-free.

Chapter 15:
Dealing with Items
You Love

Chapter 15: Dealing with Items You Love

Watching your kids grow or losing a loved one are some of the most emotional events in our lives. There is an indescribable joy that you experience when you see your kid take his first step or bring home a drawing of the family during the kindergarten years. These experiences slowly become memories, and the only way to recall these memories is to take a look at an item that is connected to them.

The same applies to the loss of a loved one. Despite the sorrow that it may bring to you, we often hold on to the possessions of a loved one to ensure that we remember them and keep their memory alive. This process is also an essential part of moving on and accepting what has happened.

So, what happens when you need to discard something that you hold dear in your heart? The emotional attachment we have to these items makes them challenging to discard. These items are what we refer to as those with sentimental value.

Decluttering is a challenging process that involves

getting rid of a lot of things in the home. These include your clothes, electronics, shoes, and many more. The difficulty of the decluttering process multiplies anytime individuals come across such sentimental items. They are very hard to let go since they spark certain emotions and memories.

Deciding to keep these items is the usual path that people take. The problem with this choice is the simple truth that you are creating clutter in the home. Understanding that letting go is the only way to move on from the past and experience the joy of the present will help in living a better life.

If you are still in this situation and finding it difficult to let go of items of sentimental value, then it is time to find the best solutions. This chapter will assist in finding excellent ways to address the issue of sentimental clutter in your home.

Decluttering Items of Sentimental Value

1. Identify Items of Actual Value

In decluttering items of sentimental value, you are stuck with objects that you associate with memories and those that you are fond of. You can simplify the decluttering process by discarding items that you have associated with a particular memory or individual. Without these items, you can still recollect the memories as well as various features of the individual in question.

The items that you are fond of are those that are of real value to you. Objects in this category don't make up the clutter in your home.

2. Avoid Being Overwhelmed by Gifts

A lot of items that are on display on most walls and shelves in the home are gifts you received from various individuals. The idea that the person that presents these gifts wants to see it any time they visit makes it difficult to declutter. It is an unnecessary obligation you create that prevents you from ridding your home of clutter.

Adopt a new approach to how you handle gifts. Once you receive it, how you use it is entirely up to you.

3. Don't Let Guilt Determine What Items You Keep

Sentiments often feed off various emotions. Guilt is one of the feelings that boosts the sentimental value of certain items. Any object you intend to keep for its sentimental value should be out of nostalgia or love.

You should understand that feeling a profound sense of guilt about a past relationship or situation won't make things right.

4. Create Digital Memories

Sentimental objects come in different forms. The furniture from your parents' home, your children's old toys, high school pictures, and old documents make up objects of sentimental value. Regardless of the method you adopt, if you physically store them, you end up creating clutter in your storage spaces.

If you are sure no one is going to make good use of the furniture or toys you are holding on to, take a picture of the furniture or make a digital copy of your kids playing with the toys. From the pictures, you can tell the appearance of an object and recollect its physical features.

Documents and other files can be converted to a digital copy by scanning. You can then get rid of the paper clutter by shredding and disposing of it properly.

5. Learn How to Handle Clutter Created by Others

You may have excellent minimalist habits that allow you to live a clutter-free life. These habits may not necessarily align with those of your partner, roommate, or family members. In this case, you need to find a smart way to get what you want.

The famous phrase/proverb, out of sight, out of mind, has a massive impact on this situation. You and the other individual can agree on a room that they can stuff with all these items. Whatever goes on in this room is not your business.

If space is not an option, then you both

need to come to an understanding. You let them put essential items on display while the others are either sold or donated. If you are lucky, merely engaging in the decluttering of your sentimental items will rub off on your partner.

6. Some Items NEED to be Donated

Here, we are not referring to donating clothes or shoes. What you need to donate in this case are items that are of historical or educational value. Some individuals love the idea of collecting various objects, including typewriters, vinyl records, china sets, old paintings, and more.

There is a high chance you will receive some of these items if you lose a loved one. Despite not needing these items, you will often feel a compulsion to keep them around. You will be doing a lot of good if you look for organizations that will value these items more than you do.

Old paintings, historical photos, old books, and a few other items can go to a local history museum, library, or archive. All you need to do is perform in-depth research on different organizations and the objects that are of value to them.

7. Give to a Relative

Family heirlooms fall within the category of objects with sentimental value. Despite their importance, you may have no need or interest in these items. Rather than disposing of or donating the object, it is best you give it to a relative.

Discuss with other members of your extended family to find an individual that would cherish the heirloom. It is a better alternative to putting it in storage or discarding the object.

8. One Item to Represent a Collection

A simple solution to address sentimental clutter is to get rid of collections. Some gifts come in a selection of numerous items. Merely selecting one thing from the collection and giving out the rest is an excellent way to control clutter in the home. It remains possible to associate the memory to this item in the same manner as the entire collection.

9. Learn to Create a Scrapbook

Creating a scrapbook is a very straightforward process. All you need is a glue stick and a notebook to begin your project. It saves space and helps retain the memories you treasure.

Scrapbooking is a suitable option for your pictures and paper items. Cut the crucial parts of the picture or paper and glue them to the notebook. To make it more fun and more comfortable to recollect the memories, remember to add notes and descriptions on each page.

It occupies less space and doesn't require expensive supplies to start.

How to Deal With Emotional Resistance When Decluttering

When decluttering sentimental items, it is common to find yourself in a situation where your emotions prevent you from letting go. Getting yourself out of the grip of these emotions is vital if you want to go on with the decluttering process. You need to have a plan that is useful in such situations.

Creating a plan depends on what you feel will work better for you based on your personality. Notwithstanding, here are a few steps to get you out of this situation or help you create a more elaborate plan:

- You should try to envision the joy on the face of another individual when you donate these items to those in need. When you know you can make an impact on the life of another person, it often creates a sense of comfort inside you.
- Look for something better to replace the item. This process fulfills the idea of keeping the best and getting rid of others. If you find yourself emotionally inclined to hold a birthday card from your grandmother, you can search for a handwritten letter to replace the card.
- Despite not being the physical object, keeping a digital image of a sentimental item

will go a long way in easing the emotions you feel.

- If your emotional barrier seems too strong to overcome, then it is time to call in some of your friends.
- Build your resistance by letting go of sentimental items last. By decluttering with regular clutter, you develop your ability to let go.

Your Quick Start Action Step:

On your schedule, add notes to remind you that you should create digital copies of sentimental items so they become easy to dispose of in the future. You should call different organizations that will find these items useful.

Chapter 16: Decluttering in One Day

Chapter 16: Decluttering in One Day

Don't get the wrong idea; decluttering is a process that takes a lot of time to complete. That is why, in this book, each room had a specific chapter discussing how to declutter. That was the small wins strategy, and for someone just getting into the habit of decluttering that is the most effective method.

Moving on to decluttering the entire home in one day requires an in-depth understanding of the small wins strategy. The one-day decluttering process is you putting the experience and speed you have developed while implementing the small wins strategy to work. It is also highly dependent on the fact that you have recently carried out a significant decluttering process in the home.

What to Avoid When Decluttering in One-Day

The time you require to complete a decluttering process makes it challenging to create time to fit in other chores. Any day you schedule for decluttering, there are several tasks you must ensure you don't perform. These are chores closely related to the decluttering process, so it is easy to get carried away. These include the following:

Cleaning

It is common to find clutter covered in grime or dust as you declutter the home. You must ensure you avoid the temptation to clean the house until a later time. If you are sure you want to complete the decluttering process in one day, then you can't lose any time deep cleaning the home.

Organizing

Understand that, just like decluttering, organizing your possessions takes a lot of time. Trying to reorganize items while decluttering will take your focus off your original goal. Schedule a different day to organize the home after the decluttering process.

Deep Purging

The one-day decluttering process is a surface decluttering process. It means you don't have time to spend opening all the boxes you keep in your attic or basement. If you want to perform this form of decluttering, then you should engage in the room-by-room decluttering of the home on another day.

Decluttering of Closets and Clothing

Once you set your sights on the items in your closet, you won't have any time to declutter any other area of the home that day. To avoid wasting precious time, it is best you avoid clothing and closet areas during the one-day house decluttering.

Preparation for the process

No matter how trivial it may seem, decluttering in one day requires preparation. Your preparation should extend to both the physical and mental preparation necessary for the procedure. Here are some of the steps you need to take to prepare for this day physically:

- Get boxes and label them
- Assemble the required supplies
- Timer for proper time management
- Get comfortable shoes and clothes you will wear on that day

Now that you know the things you need to prepare for the process, you must also realize that your speed matters a lot to the success of this process. You have to move quickly from one room to the other.

This goal of fast implementation is the reason for getting a timer. Set the timer to 30 minutes for each room you want to declutter. The timer will let you know when it is time to move to the next place. Assessing your progress within the 30 minutes you spent decluttering a room will help determine if you strayed from your original purpose.

A plan for how you intend to donate the items you don't need also matters. You can reach out to different organizations and thrift stores to determine the next step to take. Some of these organizations go the extra mile of coming to your doorstep to pick up the donations. For others, you can get information on how, when, and where to complete the donation.

How to Perform the One-day Decluttering

Since the process is a surface decluttering, the four-box strategy is useful for the procedure. Below is a room-by-room surface decluttering guide. The guide gives you suggestions on the items that should go into each box.

Feel free to edit and remove rooms based on your preference:

1. Dining Room

The area you should focus on is the dining table. This approach applies if family members have turned this surface into a dump for various items. Sort items on the dining table as follows:

- Move box: Items such as laptops that don't belong on this table but are comfortable to use.
- Storage box: Seasonal décor, fine china, and special linens.
- Donation box: Linen you no longer need but is in good condition, unwanted dishes, and old décor designs.
- Trash: Table linens with stains, old candles, and paperwork that needs shredding.

2. Coat Closet

- Move box: Any excess of shoes or sandals that are still in use.
- Storage box: Shoes and outerwear that is out of season.
- Donation box: Outerwear that is no longer wanted, those that are out of style, and those that no longer fit.
- Trash: Broken umbrellas and other items too damaged to use.

3. Kitchen

Countertops and tables in the kitchen should be your primary focus during the one-day decluttering session. Since the kitchen is quite important, you can allocate an additional 5 minutes solely to get rid of expired food items.

- Move: Mail, family members' personal items, and appliances that shouldn't be on the countertops.
- Storage Box: Out-of-season décor, tools, and gadgets for once in a year recipes.

- Donation Box: Food items you won't use and appliances that you don't need.
- Trash: Expired food items.

4. Living Room

The living room is one of the places that quickly gathers surface clutter. You may need to declutter this room more often than the others.

- Move: Personal belongings of family members, books you intend to read, and functional toys that are creating clutter.
- Storage Box: Out-of-season décor, toys, games, books, magazines, and movies.
- Donation Box: Games, décor you no longer need, old toys, books, and movies.
- Trash: Broken toys, old magazines or newspapers, incomplete puzzle or game sets, and old coloring books.

5. Linen Closet
    - Move: Cleaning items that don't belong in this closet.
    - Storage Box: Bed linens and towels that are in a proper package but not currently in use.
    - Donation Box: Excess bath and body products you are sure you won't use, bed linens and towels you don't want.
    - Trash: Bath and body products that are expired, old bed linens or towels, old cleaning supplies, and actual waste like plastic wrappings.
6. Bathrooms
    - Move: Excess toiletries like bath/body products, towels that can go to the linen closets, and personal belongings.
    - Storage Box: Extra bath toys.
    - Donation Box: Hairstyling tools you no longer need and bath/body products that are still usable but you don't want.

- Trash: Empty bath/body products, empty nail polish bottles, used makeup, used toilet paper rolls, soiled cleaning supplies, and broken bath toys.

7. Bedrooms

The clutter you are aiming to remove from the bedroom is those on the floor, bedside tables, and top of the dresser.

- Move: Personal belongings that don't belong in the bedroom.
- Storage Box: Out-of-season clothes.
- Donation Box: Bedroom décor that you are sure you don't need any longer.
- Trash: All items that should be thrown away, such as wrappers.

8. Storage Areas (Basement, Attic, Garage)

Home areas like the storage areas and clothes closet often require deep purging to declutter properly. Regardless, there are still some items you can remove from storage areas with the surface decluttering process.

Ensure you don't waste time deep purging these areas. Stick to the plan and perform a surface decluttering.

- Storage Box: Décor that will still be of use.
- Donation Box: Various items that have been in storage for over six months.
- Trash: Old newspapers, things that are broken beyond repair, product boxes, cardboard boxes, and other old packing materials.

Your Quick Start Action Step:

Pick a free day, like Saturday or Sunday, to engage in this decluttering session. You must mentally prepare yourself for the one-day decluttering session by shifting your targets to trash and surface clutter alone. This strategy is to ensure that you can follow through with the steps listed above.

Bonus Chapter: Decluttering Before Moving

Bonus Chapter: Decluttering Before Moving

This chapter is an essential addition that will be useful when you decide to move into a new home or apartment. Decluttering is a vital process you need to engage in to ensure you have less stress and spend less when moving.

Moving companies will charge extra if you have to add the things you don't need when packing. Paying for things you know you don't want isn't a smart decision, so you need to let go of these items before the moving date arrives. You also save yourself time and stress if you have a reduced number of possessions to unpack.

Over their lifetime, the average individual will move to a new home 11.7 times. This is based on a study carried out by the United States Census Bureau. The overall population structure and age group with increased chances of relocating in a year were the two datasets used in determining this value.

The study by the United States Census Bureau was performed in 2007 with a new study in 2014. The

2014 results were from independent research that indicated a drop in this value from 11.7 to 11.3 times.

As we have already established, decluttering is the only way to reduce the items you need to pack. The things you should focus on are the non-essentials and those that have been in your storage space for the last few months or years.

And if you wait for the last minute, then all the random things end up in boxes and garbage bags to be trucked over to the new place. It's not a pretty picture: opening the "oh what's in here?" box only to find loose change, dirty dishes, paperwork you needed last week and the shoes that disappeared during the move.

Why You Should Declutter Before a Move

There are numerous reasons why decluttering is essential before moving out of your current home. Understanding these benefits can get you into the mood to engage in the decluttering process in anticipation of this day. Some of the excellent benefits include the following:

- You save money on moving expenses.

- There are fewer items to unpack and arrange when you arrive at the new home.
- You create more space after unboxing and organizing your stuff.
- You find things that you can sell to cover a reasonable part of the moving expenses.
- Identifying things you don't need is vital and can touch the lives of others through donations.

Now that you know some of the benefits of decluttering before you move, what steps do you take to declutter?

How to Declutter Before Moving

There are steps you can take to ensure that you are making progress towards decluttering for a move. Some of the steps you should consider are given in this section:

1. Start Early

Deciding what to pack and things that need to be discarded isn't something you do when the moving company employees are at your doorstep. Give yourself ample time to properly declutter and get rid of the items you don't intend to take along. You should start the decluttering process a minimum of two weeks before the planned date.

You don't need to spend the entire day decluttering. Working 2-3 hours a day will help you make significant progress. Working on this short period of time is also an excellent strategy since it means that you won't get too tired and give in to the temptation of stuffing boxes randomly just to finish the task quickly.

2. Start Using Excesses

Shampoo, toilet paper, toiletries as well as other household goods that you purchase in large quantities should be used. If you start using them, it steadily reduces the stockpile of products you need to take with you when moving. It will be a good thing if you start running out of these items. You can then choose to buy small packages of these items if you need to.

3. Implement the Four-box Strategy

Following the explanation of this strategy in chapter 5, you take three boxes and a trash can into each room you intend to declutter. Check through the entire room, empty the drawers and closets, check underneath the beds, and examine the shelves for the different items you need to declutter.

Each item goes into one of the three boxes or the trash. One box should contain the items you intend to sell or donate, another for those that you intend to keep, and the last box for those that are moving to a different room.

4. Discard Expired Products

Go through the items in your bathroom cupboards and in your pantry to identify those that are past their expiration dates. If you are not sure of the expiry dates of certain items like spices, try to recall exactly when you bought the item.

Some spices can last several years. If you take in the scent and it seems like it has lost its potency, then you can throw it out. Foodstuffs in your refrigerator should also be checked to determine if they should be discarded.

Other items like makeup products that are still useful despite their age should still be considered. Those that you have had for years without making use of them should be discarded immediately.

5. Decide on How to Donate or Sell Items

In Chapter 3 of this book, you learned some of the best ways to donate specific items. Giving up an item to charity not only lifts a huge burden from your home, but it also makes you feel better about yourself. You also need to consider the things that you want to sell.

Hosting a garage sale may seem like a good idea, but it isn't the best alternative. In most cases, it requires a lot of energy and robs you of valuable time. It is quite common to have a low turnout with meager profits from these sales. To save yourself the trouble, visit an online platform like Craigslist to sell off some of these items quickly.

6. Use the Opportunity to Get Rid of

Excess Toys

Your kids' toys may occupy considerable storage space in the home, so you need to use any opportunity to declutter to your advantage. A creative way to snuff out the irrelevant toys in the house is to get them to pick out 10 – 15 toys that they want to play with as you pack your possessions. If towards the move or after moving they are still content with just these toys, then you can donate the packed items.

7. The Last Things You Should Declutter Are Those of Sentimental Value

You are preparing to move to another home, and the last thing you want to is to be overwhelmed by the emotions attached to sentimental items. Decluttering these items should come last on your list. Besides the feelings they cause to resurface, sentimental objects also cause time wastage due to indecision.

The sentimental items that you should consider discarding are those that you hide in a box in your storage room and those not on display. Most objects of sentimental value that you treasure are those that you put on display. These are the items you want to see daily.

Disposing objects of sentimental value is not a bad thing since it doesn't necessarily mean that you lose the memory connected with the object. One of the options available to you is the creation of a digital copy of the item. Take a picture, and you are all set.

Donating these items should be your priority. Ensure you find someone that will appreciate the value of the objects you are giving out. If an item causes pain and evokes emotions of sadness, then you really shouldn't be holding on to it. If there is no benefit to holding on to an item and it has no use in the home, then discard it.

Only items that make you smile and those that can be used offer enough value to remain with you.

8. Create Time Each Day to Rest

Starting early gives you a lot of time to

declutter before moving to a new place. Despite starting early, you need to limit the time you spend decluttering. This is because the process is exhausting physically, emotionally, and mentally.

After decluttering for the day, take time to recharge by having a conversation with friends or family, reading a book, or taking a cup of tea. Setting up this reward before you start decluttering for the day will provide a form of motivation to work.

9. Pack a Box of Necessities

This is a box that contains all the items that you will need as soon as you move into the new place. You must have one such box to prevent you from randomly opening different boxes to find things you need. Things like toiletries, hammers, nails, and a box cutter should be present in this box.

10. Organizing Boxes

Decluttering while preparing for a move involves packing boxes in preparation for the day you move. As you declutter and fill up different boxes, ensure you are putting labels on them while using tape to seal the box shut. Move the box to out of the room to create space to continue decluttering.

Choose an empty room or free space in the home where you can start stacking the boxes as you bring them out. The label on each box should indicate what room it is going to. You should also inscribe a list of the items in the box.

Quick Action Step

It is easy to read a book and forget about it once you learn and adopt the various principles given in the book. For this chapter, it is easy to overlook since it may not currently apply to your situation. To ensure you can find this chapter when it becomes necessary, create a note that refers you back to this book when you need to prepare for a move.

Conclusion

Clutter consists of anything that you can quickly identify as trash in the home. Understanding that other regular items in the house identify as clutter is the reason you can conclude that you have a clutter problem in the home. A clutter problem has a significant impact both physically and mentally making it vital that you eliminate clutter in your home.

Decluttering is the process you adopt to rid your home of clutter effectively. It is a process that can take a bit of time but is well worth it in the end. Decluttering is not something you jump into. It requires a lot of changes in your life. First, you have to develop a mindset to properly implement this process while also developing the discipline to ensure that you can keep up with the demands of the process.

If you are feeling down and incompetent just because your home is filled with clutter, you are far from the truth. According to various stats on clutter, a significant percentage of homes around the world face a similar problem. Although it can be attributed to the consumerist lifestyle, you must focus more on the solution rather than beating yourself up.

The different chapters in this book have given an insight into some of the vital aspects of decluttering that you would benefit beneficial to your home decluttering efforts. From the importance of focusing on small wins, you find out about how this strategy can help you overcome the feeling of being overwhelmed anytime you face the clutter in your home. It also extends to the importance of donating some of your items and where these items will be better appreciated.

The idea of focusing on small wins is very significant when considering how to declutter each room in the home. Certain rooms are much more comfortable to declutter than others, and you learn the reason for this as you read through. Areas like the kitchen, bathroom, laundry room, garage, attic, and basement are spaces that require the divide and conquer approach to decluttering. In these areas, the clutter you need to declutter often requires additional time compared to other areas of the home.

This book promised to provide a step-by-step guide on how to declutter the home. Since decluttering is a process that you don't just jump into, you need to create a plan on how to go about it. By offering key steps that are effective in decluttering specific rooms in the home, you have the upper hand in ridding the home of clutter.

A particular chapter dedicated to decluttering sentimental items offers an in-depth look at the solution to one of the most significant problems individuals face during the decluttering process. Some tips can help you get over the emotions associated with sentimental items, as well as excellent ways on how to keep the memories attached to these items alive without having to depend on their physical presence.

If there is anything that you must take away from this book, then you must understand the importance of small wins. Your focus on small wins is an approach to clutter problems that you can use, as well as for your other life endeavors. Through this approach, you learn that when tackling a problem that seems overwhelming, all you need to do is break it down into smaller parts that are easier to handle.

After completing a small part of the task, you celebrate your small win to gain motivation to move on to the next task. Repeating this process will get you to the finish line in a more straightforward manner than if you attempt to go big on the first try. If there is one thing you should take home from this book, it's that with consistent effort you can have a beautiful decluttered home to enjoy!

References

35 Surprising Home Organization Statistics That'll Inspire You to Tidy Up. (2019). Retrieved from https://www.organizedinteriors.com/blog/home-organization-statistics/

Babauta, L. (2013). Declutter Your Life : zen habits. Retrieved from https://zenhabits.net/declutter/

Browne, K. (2019). Strategies to Let Go of Sentimental Items. Retrieved from https://www.getorganizedwizard.com/blog/2019/03/strategies-to-let-go-of-sentimental-items/

Ewer, C. (2019). Declutter 101: Strategies To Cut Clutter | Organized Home. Retrieved from https://organizedhome.com/cut-clutter/declutter-101-strategies-cut-clutter

How To Declutter Your Books - Tale Away. (2019). Retrieved from http://taleaway.com/how-to-declutter-your-books/

How to Declutter Your Home in One Day. (2018).

Retrieved from https://www.showmesuburban.com/how-to-declutter-your-house-in-one-day/

How to Declutter Your Home: A Ridiculously Thorough Guide | Budget Dumpster. (2019). Retrieved from https://www.budgetdumpster.com/resources/how-to-declutter-your-home.php#garage

Hudson, K. (2019). What are small wins?. Retrieved from http://smallwinsinnovation.com/small-wins/

Jones, R. (2017). Tips to Declutter Your Home Before a Move - Nourishing Minimalism. Retrieved from https://nourishingminimalism.com/blog/declutter-your-home-before-move/

Larkin, E. (2019). A Foolproof Method for Decluttering Your Home. Retrieved from https://www.thespruce.com/decluttering-your-entire-home-2648002

Lawson, A. (2019). Organizing Books with the KonMari Method. Retrieved from https://justagirlandherblog.com/the-konmari-method-organizing-books/

Rodgers, H. (2013). Day 21: Fridge {31 Days of Easy Decluttering}. Retrieved from http://www.fromoverwhelmedtoorganizedblog.com/2013/10/day-21-fridge-31-days-of-easy.html

Rodgers, H. (2013). Day 13: Pantry {31 Days of Easy Decluttering}. Retrieved from http://www.fromoverwhelmedtoorganizedblog.com/2013/10/day-13-pantry-31-days-of-easy.html

Russell, M. (2019). How to Declutter your Storage Room without Feeling Overwhelmed - Simple Lionheart Life. Retrieved from https://simplelionheartlife.com/declutter-your-storage-room/

Stillman, J. (2015). 5 Steps to Get the Right Mindset for Success. Retrieved from https://www.inc.com/jessica-stillman/5-steps-to-get-the-right-mindset-for-success.html

Yang, S. (2016). https://www.realsimple.com. Retrieved from https://www.realsimple.com/home-organizing/organizing/declutter-garage

Declutter Your Life:

Simple Decluttering Strategies on How to Declutter and Organize your Life to Free Yourself from Worry and Enjoy Stress-Free Living

Madeline Crawford

Introduction:

We often relate clutter mainly to material things. We see clothing placed over the dresser, on top of the treadmill, and covering other available surfaces in the bedroom. Then we see magazines and books scattered across the coffee table and extra dishes stacked on the counter.

In truth, clutter can also be a social, emotional, and mental issue. The demands we face every day can lead to an increase in stress at a point in our lives.

Various aspects of our lives can become overwhelming, leading to struggles from financial mismanagement to home clutter to messy schedules that seem to be impossible to get organized. You may need to address a different type of clutter if your mind is busy with various thoughts. Or are tired because of a full weekly schedule that prevents you from sleeping adequately.

If your goal is to declutter, it's crucial to keep in

mind that there are valid reasons that allow for the buildup of material things. It's in human nature to get disorganized from time to time. We are more likely to get disorganized during our busy lives, such as moving into a new house or being tied up in a big project at school or work.

The buildup will inevitably occur despite our best efforts to prevent clutter from happening, and this is entirely normal. When it comes to our degree of tolerance toward clutter, we all differ. You must always be diligent about picking up and staying organized because it's hard to declutter once your lack of order becomes notorious.

One of the main reasons for the difficulty of decluttering is that we find it hard to let go of things. The way hoarders feel when they give away objects with which they have formed an attachment is similar to the feeling of physical pain. Studies have shown that giving others our prized possessions activated the same area in our brain that recognizes pain. In other words, giving things away literally hurts. We become more attached to an object as we spend more time with it.

Being disorganized or cluttered is a normal part of life, while hoarding is a physiological disorder. In non-hoarders, the neurological reaction to giving things away is much less intense than that of hoarders. The response is still present, though, so it's worth pointing out.

Having this in the back of your mind will make it easier for you to get rid of things. You will find yourself in situations where you want to keep something because you feel attached to it. In these instances, you should assess to determine the validity of your attachment by asking yourself whether you are indeed connected to it or if you are considering the pain that comes with losing that item.

There is a theory that asserts that clutter is the symptom of indecisiveness. Struggling with indecision can be the result of growing up in a home where no item was ever discarded or having difficulties revolving around making the right choice. Regardless of its origin, your indecision may make it very difficult for you to figure out whether to keep an object or not. You instead tend to forego that decision by merely holding on to that object, thereby surpassing making a decision altogether.

When it comes to decluttering, the reason for keeping an item is more important than the object itself.

In later chapters, we will be discussing this in more detail and providing solutions.

The famous duo known as "The Minimalists" says that the reason for our clutter is more important than how we clutter. They associate clutter with a consumerist mindset which has become a feature of modern society. When decluttering, it helps to understand the basics of minimalism as well as its practice to distinguish between necessary and unnecessary items.

There is a saying by Albert Einstein that goes as follows: "If a cluttered desk is a sign of a cluttered mind, of what, then, is an empty desk a sign?"

This quote is an intriguing point that several people have taken to heart. Most people believe very creative and highly intelligent individuals work from messy desks or reside in messy houses.

There's some truth in the great Einstein's

statement1 showed that people found it easier to come up with solutions to a creative challenge when they were in a messy area than in an organized one. A lot of people jokingly use this to justify messy workplaces, but as with most things in life, there's more underneath the surface.

In a different study,2). Only 47 percent of those participants that were in the disorganized room donated, while 87 percent of people that were in the cleanroom donated. The final part of the experiment involved offering each participant the choice of candy or an apple on their way out. Can you guess who chose the apple? The people from the cleanroom were more than three times as likely to opt for a healthy choice.

So, what have we learned from these studies? While disorderliness increases your creative capabilities, cleanliness encourages you to make the right decisions. Other conclusions can be drawn from different results. A study found that interested and curious individuals and people with many interests were more likely to be disorganized. In reality, these results may have more to do with the type of people involved in the study than the state of their surroundings.

Every one of us has an optimum work environment. For some people, this can be a clear desk with a laptop, a pen, and a notepad. For other people, it is a kitchen table filled with a few printouts, some books, a couple of handouts, a laptop, a water bottle, and a cup of coffee. This setup goes beyond your home and your workspace. Some people feel good when everything around them is orderly and clean, while others may feel that decluttering every day is a bit excessive.

The most important thing you can do is find your best balance. This sweet spot also applies to your spouse if you have one. Doing this reduces stress. Take a second and think about your digital workspace. You make life easier for yourself by clearing your inbox and decluttering your browser tabs and your desktop. Doing this will force you back up old but essential files. You can even find things you thought you had lost, such as past articles in Pocket, or rediscover some old notes on Evernote. You can inject new energy into your life through digital decluttering.

I firmly believe material possessions do not equate to happiness. This belief made me try out the idea of minimalistic living. I wanted to see if I would obtain a less cluttered mind if I spent time in a less cluttered home.

I made decluttering every aspect of my life my priority and achieved my goals by getting rid of all the things I felt were unnecessary. Doing this reduced the number of my material possessions, which in turn helped me focus on my most valuable items.

Take a look below at the seven steps I followed to declutter my belongings:

- **Step 1**: I sorted my possessions into their appropriate categories, such as shoes, jewelry, clothes, cosmetics, books, electronics, bags, and so on.

- **Step 2**: I took out everything from one category so that I could have an idea of the number of items within the category as well as the category's size compared to others.

- **Step 3**: I got rid of any items that immediately seemed unnecessary.

- **Step 4**: I carefully worked my way through the remaining items, and I discarded anything I didn't need or the things I didn't love.

- **Step 5**: This was a tough call, and I needed to face it without unnecessary sentiments. I removed items in my "keep pile" after further consideration as to whether I loved them or not.

- **Step 6**: I organized the items I decided to keep.

- **Step 7**: I gave away the items that didn't make the "keep pile" to charity shops, friends, and recycling centers.

Clutter can be a significant energy drain or a severe waste of time for most people, as it makes it challenging to locate what they need. In extreme cases, clutter can be a cause of depression or even of obesity, especially when a life of consumption goes beyond just stuff. A cluttered house can cause health complications due to the accumulation of dust and mold, and clutter can cause fire hazards, especially in situations where a person is a hoarder. However, extreme cases are not very common.

Here is a bit of good news for you: decluttering can become more straightforward and less time consuming, producing little or no physical or emotional stress. Many lessons are learned while decluttering, and the sense of achievement and control that come at the end of the process can be a significant stress reliever.

By discarding unnecessary items, you may free up much-needed space at home. It is also helpful to declutter before you move to a new house. The decluttering strategies you are going to encounter in this comprehensive guide will assist you on your journey toward a clutter-free life.

In this book, you will find detailed solutions on how to declutter and simplify your life. These solutions also include organizing your activities, finances, and even your digital files, all aimed to help you live a decluttered, stress-free life.

Chapter 1: Declutter Your Life - The Starting Point

Chapter 1: Declutter Your Life - The Starting Point

There's a common misconception that clutter only relates to physical items. When we think of clutter, we visualize magazines and books scattered on the coffee table, clothes tossed in weird places, or extra dishes on the counter. The truth is that clutter can also manifest as a social, emotional, or mental issue.

You have a cluttered mind when it is filled with competing thoughts, and this can affect your sleep. You may also be exhausted after hectic weekly schedules. This issue certainly isn't physical clutter, but rather clutter in another form.

To accurately define clutter as what it is, you need to know what it is not. Clutter is not the same thing as dirt. Even the neatest housekeepers can have clutter accumulating on their desks and shelves.

Clutter and hoarding are two different things. Clutter is something that happens when you unintentionally collect items throughout your home or space. Hoarding, on the other hand, is the unhealthy process of holding on to unnecessary stuff. All that is needed to correct clutter is being committed to the organization, while hoarding may need external intervention to be fixed.

Clutter does not include collecting valuable items. My aunt collects ends and odds from around the world. Her house is full of collectibles, yet it doesn't feel cluttered, and this is because she displays them on shelves or in cabinets. Things aren't laying around in areas of frequent use such as kitchen counters or walkways.

The Origin of Clutter

You would look for and close off the source of a leak in the basement before you start collecting the water, right? With that in mind, let's familiarize ourselves with the way clutter forms before we begin to look at ways to get rid of it. When it comes to clutter, everyone living in a home contributes to its accumulation, especially the little ones. Kids drag home small items from their meals or parties, and they leave their toys out.

Like kids, adults also generate clutter. This clutter usually happens when we feel we're too busy to return an object to its rightful place. The result is leaving it anywhere that is convenient at that moment, like the dining table.

These items gradually accumulate, and in no time, a small pile becomes a sizeable one. Catalogs, junk mail, and magazine subscriptions are another means through which we gain clutter.

By recognizing the role you play in accumulating clutter, you are a step closer to reducing it. Failure to accept responsibilities is one of the things that hinders the decluttering process at home. Families spend their time blaming one another for the clutter instead of taking the fact that everyone plays a role, then moving forward toward a solution.

Definition of "Clutter" and "Decluttering"

The words "decluttering" and "clutter" often appear with one another, but what do they mean? It's essential to know the meaning of these terms, as they form the basis of the problem this book aims to solve.

My idea of physical clutter is items that do the following:

- make your space messy or disordered;

- are unnecessary and don't contribute to your happiness

- they keep postponing your decision on what to do with them.

In my opinion, clutter is a symptom, not a cause; it is a symptom of the inability to make the right decisions (or any decisions for that matter) concerning the items in your space. There are many reasons for this. You may find it hard because it's an emotional decision, or you may have a hectic schedule and finding it hard to find the time needed to put things in order.

Decluttering is the process by which you determine whether items in your space are clutter, and you decide to put the necessary things in the right place. By helping you understand the reason there's clutter in the first place, decluttering allows you to make the permanent changes required. Hoarding Disorders UK have a useful measure of information on clutter found on their website. The image scale on the site helps viewers determine the condition of their space by picking the picture in the sequence that closely resembles the situations in their rooms.

According to Hoarding Disorders UK, having things around you might reach a point where it starts to encroach on other people's lives to the point where you might have to seek help for your hoarding problem When it comes to clutter, the most critical aspect is how you feel about your space. We all have different ideas of what we consider to be clutter. For some people, something like a few clothes on a chair makes them feel like their home is cluttered. For some, they begin to feel their space is cluttered when piled-up objects start to limit their movements within the house.

One thing people who want to declutter have in common is the overwhelming feeling that comes from cluttered space. Ideally, your home should be a place that reduces your stress levels - a place where you can breathe easily. Your workspace should be a location where you feel productive, efficient, and in control (to a certain degree).

Importance of Decluttering Your Life

There are many benefits to decluttering than meets the eye; it has significant positive effects on your mind, body, and the world at large. Hearing this may be the push you need to get started. Read on and prime yourself for decluttering.

1. **Purifies the air around you**. Clutter attracts dust, and this reduces the purity of the air you breathe in. Few things do as much good for your body and mind as some spring (or summer, fall, or winter) cleaning. It purifies the air around you.

2. **Mind sharpening**. A Princeton University study found that the brain's ability to focus improves as you declutter your living and working spaces3. In simple terms, by having fewer things to divert your attention to, such as clutter, you have a more productive mind for concentrating on the task at hand.

3. **Eliminates negative energy**. A common place to find clutter is in a room behind closed doors. The reason is this room is something no one wants to see, yet everyone in the house knows it is there. It becomes taboo to talk about this spare room. Here's the thing - everything gives off either positive or negative

energy. The question is, which one do you want more?

4. **It makes room for promising opportunities**. Everyone wants better things coming in their lives, but these things are blocked by some of the old stuff we won't do away with. For example, you would love to bring in new clients for your business, but your workspace is filled with paper, garbage, and old files. New clients can't come if the old stuff remains there.

5. **It makes you money**. Who doesn't want to have more money? The money you so deserve is probably right in front of you in the form of the heap of stuff in your garage, spare room, or attic. By selling these things, you could make enough money to take a friend out for dinner, take a short vacation, pay off a little debt, open a savings account, or pay for anything else you can imagine.

6. **Mindful purchasing**. When we make purchases, it is usually on a whim. This action is a waste of hard-earned money because we

aren't considering whether we need or like such items. By decluttering, we develop a mindset that directs us to make better decisions when it comes to purchasing things.

7. **Money saved from unnecessary and frivolous purchases**. You can save a lot of money by limiting your purchases to only the items you feel are necessary. You'll be surprised to find out that the group of items you spend the most money on can be clothing. By reducing your clothes shopping, you will have more money in your pocket to do the things you love.

8. **Creativity stimulation**. Removing excess clutter from your space stimulates your creativity. It also calms your mind, and this makes it easier for you to create beautiful works. Give your creativity a boost by tidying your environment.

9. **Save time by being able to find things more easily**. Your time is precious, and it probably shouldn't be spent hunting through pile after pile of stuff just to find any

item you are looking for. By reducing your possessions, you can find things faster and spend less time looking for them. This approach is better than rooting through hangers of clothes or diving into a mountain of handbags just to find a specific one.

10. **Space is saved from owning less**. The amount of storage space you need increases with the number of materials you possess. You may discover you need about half of your space after decluttering. This discovery may prompt you to get a smaller apartment. This move would be more economical than your current area, which may be bigger than what you need.

11. **Happier outlook**. You feel more satisfied when you surround yourself with items that are precious to you. Undesirable items will no longer cover your favorite things or lodged in strange places like the bottom of the drawer or behind the cupboard. Your favorite items do not need to be reserved for only special occasions. They can and should be

out in the open all the time for you to see and use freely. This approach will most certainly make you a happier person.

12. **Quicker and more accessible to clean and tidy**. It is much easier to clean a house with few possessions than it is to clean one filled with clutter. Every item has a place, and it is best if you know exactly where to find everything. You can only achieve this by reducing the number of your possessions. Your mind will be less cluttered once your living space is tidier.

13. **More freedom**. A sense of freedom and lightness awaits you when you place greater importance on experiences than materials and let go of material possessions. You can get addicted to the wonderful sense of freedom that comes with being rid of suffocating and unnecessary materials. By detaching yourself from possessions, you can shift your focus to better things like experiences and people.

14. **Promotes relaxation**. Your stress

levels at home are at their peak when you are dealing with belongings. By reducing the amount of time spent dealing with your stuff, you can significantly reduce your stress levels. Applying this habit also helps you to become a calmer individual.

15. **Move forward already**. That box containing cards, letters, trinkets, and so on from your ex-boyfriend or ex-girlfriend is only going to hold you back. Face it - you got hurt and they aren't coming back so why do you keep holding on to those things? Let it go! Accept it, and move on with your life. You must love tormenting yourself if you choose to keep reading those old letters, and it's awful for your mental health, so you should stop doing so.

16. **You are helping others**. You don't have to throw out your unnecessary items, because they may be useful to someone else. Make sure to think about whether the things you are considering throwing away can be donated to a business or thrift store to help out someone else and prevent waste.

17. **Get the monkey off your back**. This monkey goes by a familiar name: clutter. He sits on your back, and he pokes you very hard from time to time. As you have imagined, he is very annoying. He times his pokes at the exact moment you walk by the garage and other places that have accumulated stuff. As if poking you wasn't infuriating enough, he laughs hysterically at you, because he knows you are not going to do a thing about that mess. Haven't you had enough of him? His taunts only raise your stress levels. Since he weighs a ton, he makes your steps heavier than they should be. Get rid of him so that you can be light on your feet.

Decluttering Myths Debunked

Decluttering could be done in more than one way and leads to organizing space. Practices and methods of decluttering that work for one person might not work for another without some modifications. And just like everything, decluttering also has its myth. Below is a list of popular decluttering myths.

Myth #1: You must be organized every day

of the week.

The truth: No matter how organized you are, the gathering of clutter (no matter how little) is inevitable in life.

At times, you may need to rest instead of cleaning up because you have had a long and stressful day. It's okay. Give yourself a little break and take care of your cleaning chores the following day. You would most likely do a more efficient job organizing with your batteries recharged.

Having a routine and schedule is the key that allows you to maintain a neat home without worrying about decluttering or feeling burnt out. Impossibly high standards of organization would only cause disappointment and frustration.

Myth #2: Decluttering only needs to be done once in a while.

The truth: The process of decluttering is an ongoing and regular process.

You would be free from the disorganized and burdensome feeling associated with living in a cluttered home if you must invest time in a major decluttering project. Although working to reduce the clutter is an excellent first step. A focused effort to declutter once a year isn't enough.

A schedule for regular decluttering is the only way of consistently having a neat home and organized life. Endeavor to set time for this task weekly. Give a little more time to your cleaning and decluttering tasks once regularly.

Myth #3: Having an empty space is a bad thing.

The truth: At times, it is about what is not present when it comes to what a room looks like to you.

Maybe it is the negative meaning of the word 'empty' which shows an empty space as a bad thing.

The term "negative space" from the art world has been borrowed by some interior decorators to describe spaces in the home intentionally unoccupied by furniture or even artwork on the walls. It is no wonder the concept gets a bad reputation as "negative" is attached to its name.

Decluttering does not only entail removing junk

and cleaning up. It could also include intentionally keeping space or spaces empty while making decorating choices. That serves a few objectives.

First, a less occupied space could induce calm and not be too much for our brains. Our attention could also be drawn to other items as well as features present in the room, which becomes more pronounced in empty spaces.

"Clutter" does not only indicate piles of useless things. It could also be putting too many things on the walls or corners. The island and table are more pronounced due to the intentional use of empty space.

Myth #4: A messy individual is unable to change their poor organization habits.

The truth: This is a decluttering myth that we can refer to as nonsense.

Being a well-organized individual is not a character or a trait; it is actually a skill. And like every skill, organizational skills can be learned, and it can build up over time depending on the individual's patience and will to build the capability.

If you consider figurative expressions like "you

can't teach an old dog new tricks," or "a leopard can't change its spots," it appears that it might be a bit difficult to get an older person to become neat all of a sudden.

However, if you consider an expression like "if you're not learning you're not living," and many more words of wisdom concerning learning, it is possible for positive change.

Myth #5: The way to go is to live a minimalist lifestyle.

The truth: It does not apply to everyone.

Many people have been taught to live with fewer things, with media articles advising to re-examine our consumerist inclination. However, not everyone sees enjoyment as an include extreme and sudden downsizing to live in a small shipping container, micro condo, or tiny home.

Having more things not needed by you does not make you worse than someone practicing the minimalist lifestyle. It all boils down to personal preference.

Ensure that you do not buy too many things which

leads to you drowning in clutter. Buy the things you need only, and not just the item you want, or things you think you need. There is a saying which thus "Own your things, don't let your things own you."

Myth #6: You can remain organized without some extra help.

The truth: Many great organization helpers exist all over the world. Make proper use of them.

The variation of these common decluttering myths is that you are capable of keeping a neat home without spending money on storage systems as well as a quality organization.

Correct, it can be done, but why not make it easier for yourself?

There are lots of wonderful products available (such as bed surrounds and closet organizers) which are explicitly designed to increase storage space and prevent time-wasting. These tools make it less challenging to stay organized.

Although these useful tools do not do all the work in keeping you organized, they make it easier for you to stay organized. There are various great products which can help you to stay organized with little effort, take advantage of it.

Myth #7: It is manageable to live with clutter.

The truth: Indeed, you can technically live a chaotic life and get used to the clutter surrounding you. However, the longer you leave your clutter, the more your life becomes unmanageable.

Think about the time wasted every day when searching for items in a disorganized office or home. In addition to the causes of time-wasting clutter, it can also lead to poor sleeping habits and stress, as well as other medical problems.

Step-by-Step Strategy on How to Declutter Your Life and Lower Stress Levels

Deciding to declutter your home is not an easy task, and its difficulty can sometimes make it unappealing to attempt. Decluttering is no different from other things in life in that the hardest part is getting started. Listed below are reliable decluttering tips that will aid you as you begin to regain control of your space by clearing clutter.

Step 1: Set goals. Having a plan before you begin an activity goes a long way in making the whole process easier for you. Specific goals will help to tackle decluttering, regardless of the amount of clutter you have ahead of you. Below are some of the things you should consider before deciding to declutter your home:

- Make physical notes or draw up a map showing clutter within the house.

- Give each room a grade based on the clutter within that space. For example, you can use a scale of 1-3 with 3 being highest; a messy closet or room would be a 3. This grading system helps you prioritize your time.

- Visualize your goal (in this case, your dream room) before you begin. Take note of its details, use, and the placement of your possessions. Let your vision direct your decluttering efforts. If you come across a lovely picture online or in a magazine, try to reproduce the feel of it in your own space. The more specific your vision, the higher your level of motivation.

- Schedule deadlines for the completion of each phase of your cleanup. To avoid frustration, make your deadlines attainable. Decluttering can be fun if you challenge yourself.

- To complement your completion dates, have plans to tackle the specific areas with the highest amount of clutter, like a garage or basement. These areas may require more than a couple of hours to declutter.

Step 2: Create a sorting system. A sorting system is necessary for your decluttering to be effective. You can come up with your own method, or you can use the "Three-Box Method," which happens to be one of the most organizational strategies. What this method does is it puts you in a situation whereby you must make a single decision on the fate of every single item in your possession.

Get three boxes or storage bins, and label them as detailed using the guide below:

- **"Keep" box.** You empty this box when you complete a space. The items from this box should go to designated locations in your home. You should store them neatly in a drawer or container, and label them if you so desire.

- **"Get rid of" box.** As with the previous box, empty this one when you are done with the area. Put any items you want to sell or give away into this box. If you don't have a storage space, keep them in the vehicle you plan on using to transport them to a store. They can also temporarily go in the attic or garage.

- **"Put in storage" box.** Put the contents of this box in storage containers, label the containers or place an inventory sheet on them, and arrange them neatly in your storage area.

Step 3: Get mentally prepared. Decluttering is a time-consuming process, and accepting this fact will make your journey easier. The clutter you are clearing didn't appear overnight, so it can't be handled in an instant. Always keep this in mind: small steps in the proper direction still count as steps in the appropriate direction. You will gradually move toward your objectives.

- **Until you are done decluttering, try not to bring new things into your home.** You do not want to add to your considerable workload by bringing home new items.

- **Ask yourself the right questions.** You need to ask yourself this when you come across an item while decluttering: Does this spark joy? This practical question has its downsides. For most people, it can be a trap, because they find ways to justify keeping items that make them happy, even if they rarely use them.

A practical and straightforward mantra to decide on what things to give up or keep is "use it, cherish it, or let it go". Do you use it frequently? Do you cherish it, or does it help to make your life better in a way (such as photographs, souvenirs, or artwork)? If your answers in response to all these questions are negative, then that item should not go in the keep pile.

- **Keep your vision in mind and follow through with it.** Always have the image of your desired room in mind as you declutter. When you find yourself struggling with decisions on your possessions, ask yourself these two questions:

  o What's presently in the space that would take me away from my vision?

  o What's in my space right now that will bring the room closer to my vision?

- **If the decluttering becomes difficult, continue to persevere by using your motto.** Decision fatigue is going to set in at some point, and that's okay. Instead of giving up, use a mantra. Here are some effective mantras to keep you going when things get tough and to remind you why you're decluttering:

  o If you keep too much, you can't find what's essential.

- Your desk is a work surface, not a storage area.

- Your bed is a space for sleeping, not a dirty clothes hamper.

- Your nightstand is home to your lamp and a couple of books; it's not a medicine cabinet.

Step 4: Start sorting

- **Tackle one room or one space at a time.** It's most effective to start with the place that is bothering you the most, whether it's the junk drawer, garage, bedroom closet, or kitchen. By taking on the room that causes the most significant spike in your stress levels and makes you want to run away, you build up the motivation and momentum needed to follow the task through to the end. You can also achieve the same effect by primarily working on the space that affects your daily life the most.

- **Start with what you can see.** You've marked your problem area, so now you should gradually begin decluttering by working on the items you can see. These are visible surfaces like desktops, tables, floor space, or the tops of dressers. After handling these, you can move on to deeper regions, like cabinets and drawers.

- **Don't forget to focus on the big stuff, too.** It's easy to ignore the big stuff when you are faced with little things like the items scattered on the bookshelf. Big things can create even more chaos than the small stuff. Furniture placement, for example, can be a form of visual clutter and may make long-term organization difficult.

If you have too many unused large toys or furniture in a single room, you should move these items out. You can give yourself a motivation boost by reorganizing your space. Clutter also ruins your sleep, and nobody wants that.

- **Declutter one item at a time.** Clutter is the result of deferred decision making, so it is better to handle things one at a time to make reasonable progress.

- **Turn sentimental items into stories.** Sentimental items can be tough to part with. However, with a simple strategy, you can make what is usually a tough decision a bit easier. Simply take a picture of the item, and write an accompanying story about its history and significance. This picture and its emotional message are more precious than an item you no longer use. You also need to consider the fact that the person who gave you such an item wouldn't want it being a burden to you.

- **Give everything a home.** Finding a specific space for each item goes a long way in ensuring clutter doesn't accumulate again. If you are unable to allocate a designated area for an object, continue reducing your things until you find one.

- **Seek assistance from an expert.** You can always reach out to a professional organizer if you have trouble decluttering. Obtaining expert advice during the decluttering and organizational process will immensely increase your chances of getting the job done.

You can also schedule a pickup when you have figured out the items you will want to store.

Step 5: Get rid of the clutter. You have a couple of options when it comes to disposing of the items in the "get rid of it" box.

- **Recycle.** Recyclable paper, glass, and plastics can go in the recycling bin if you have curbside pickup. If not, your recyclables should go into a bag so that you can take them to the closest recycling center to you.

A lot of electronic gadgets should be recycled. There are over 1,890 EcoATM recycling kiosks in 42 states. These kiosks give you cash from your old electronics. Check prices for your old devices, and use the ecoATM locator to find the nearest one to you.

- **Donate or freecycle.** It is refreshing to know your unwanted item will be transferred to a new home. Shoes, clothes, and other household pieces in proper form can be given as donations to a local charity of your choice as long you follow the charity's donation guidelines.

You also have the option of making a post on freecycle.org. You can post the things you want to dispose of and people, can come and pick up the items. What you regard as trash might be very valuable to someone else.

- **Have a garage sale.** You can make money off your clutter if you are up to the challenge. You can do this by having a garage sale. Check if your neighborhood or homeowner's association has a garage sale date set aside. You should start your decluttering early so that you have enough items to display at the sale. By having a lot of goods shown, you will have more foot traffic, and this usually results in more sales.

- **Rent a dumpster.** This option is a very affordable and stress-free one for those who have a lot of items to get rid of. It can also be used by people who want to dispose of large household items. If you rent a dumpster, your only task is to fill their vehicle up with your unwanted items. They will haul it away when you are done. It's that simple!

Your Quick Start Action Step:

1. Look around your house and assess the level of disorganization.
2. Think of the areas in your house that need to be organized.
3. Evaluate your life and list areas that need to be organized.
4. Picture how those places in your house and areas in your life will look like after you organize.
5. Write down the benefits you'll gain after you organize.

Chapter 2: Proper Mindset when Decluttering Your Life

Chapter 2: Proper Mindset When Decluttering Your Life

Your frame of mind encompasses the entirety of your knowledge. These include your values and opinions about life and your role in it. It helps you sort through every piece of information you come across and determine what is useful and what is not. Hence, it influences the way you take in knowledge as well as respond to it.

More often than not, having the proper mindset for the choices you make is the most significant factor. Cultivating the appropriate mindset is essential to excel in anything at all. Subsequently, you create the values that are most beneficial for your purpose or ambition. This system of belief is therefore referred to as your mindset.

We will assume that an abundant mindset will portray authenticity and help you. The arrangement has to be something like this:

- Identify the most helpful beliefs and values.

- Determine those beliefs that agree with

(a possible) reality.

It is good that you channel your mindset into something productive; this explains why your beliefs and values don't have to portray your present situation. However, the reality that you hold to be valid must be achievable. It is like a catch-22, but not exactly.

If you think you're well-coordinated, you will act accordingly. If you believe you wish to be a well-organized person, you must act equally accordingly - like an unorganized person.

The idea of embracing a seemingly difficult belief is impressive, because it affects your mindset, and ultimately, how you act, in a positive way. It allows growth. If you desire to do anything remarkable at all, you must then cultivate the habit of following through.

This approach is where most of us falter because acting on it is daunting. It will cost you the habit of persistence necessary to carry out your lifestyle goals. You also need to be daring enough to set giant, intimidating goals and then tell those who you can share it with that you will achieve these goals.

You must have the courage to claim a piece of the pie for yourself. Additionally, it takes endurance and persistence - a lot of it. At the same time, a great deal of hard work is required before you will ever benefit from the time and effort you may have invested. This action runs the risk of becoming extremely frustrating, but in the end, it could provide lasting benefits.

You may be wondering what the way out is. It is forming the habit of endurance better than anyone else around you and enjoying the grueling work, regardless of what anyone else advises. This outlook becomes a positive mindset to achieve your personal goal.

Any gainful course requires endurance, but when the goal is achieved, the means are justified.

What makes having the right mindset so important?

If you are truly determined to be successful in any of your endeavors, then you definitely must learn how to develop the right mindset for the reasons that are mentioned below.

1. It is building a healthy self-esteem. To achieve anything meaningful, a person must first be confident of the fact that he can accomplish it, whether everybody agrees or not. Self-esteem emanates from an inner conversation that determines what price we place on our worth, as well as how we see ourselves. Also, it forms the general idea we have of ourselves.

A positive and strong mindset is vital in developing healthy self-esteem. It affects our everyday self-talk and reinforces the feelings, beliefs, and attitudes that we hold dear to us. So, manage your state of mind by planting seeds of inspiration and positivity instead of criticizing and doubting yourself

2. Creating a success perspective. When success is involved, several aspects are more critical to reaching this perspective. The importance attached to events and situations has an intense effect on how you view things, such as, for instance, seeing a glass as either half empty or half full. In life, nothing has an inherent meaning except that which is given to it.

The truth is, your state of mind has absolutely everything to do with your perception of life. The beliefs formed early in life, your manner of approach, and your prejudices automatically influence your response to details as well as how you view the world around you. Keeping a positive outlook on life increases the chances of creating a success perspective and of obtaining lasting success.

3. You are channeling your drive. Drive refers to a stubborn resolve to accomplish a vital objective. It involves the process of creating a mental picture of success and maintaining a constant effort over time. When the drive is absent, it will be almost impossible to achieve most objectives.

Your mindset is vital to your drive. When channeled and focused on a lasting purpose, you can propel yourself toward above your present status. It also means that you move beyond the settled method of doing things that requires little effort and yield only barely acceptable results.

Those who have passion are self-motivated and do their best to achieve more. These people do not laze around complaining about their circumstances or give excuses; instead, they focus on improving their situation.

4. Being faced with adversity. It doesn't matter what you are out to accomplish; you will experience some level of trouble and hardships on the road to success. Nevertheless, if you wish to survive the difficulties, you will learn to develop resistance and deal with each challenge with everything you've got.

It is at this juncture that your mindset comes to play. Adversity tries one's courage to the crux. After being faced with tremendous difficulty, an individual might feel like he or she has every reason to throw in the towel. To such people, that might appear to be the easiest way out. Nonetheless, the ability to pass through fire and be battered but not defeated is a genuine proof of a resilient mindset.

5. Accomplishing the fundamental objectives. Goal-setting is a many-sided process, with accomplishment being the most palpable gauge for success. However, in the absence of the right mindset, you may end up not making it to that point. Accomplishing a target requires a better-than-average desire to achieve something.

Mindset is the point where your resiliencies are being put to the test. Mental toughness is what determines the likelihood of someone pushing beyond the surface to succeed despite the hardships being faced or merely succumbing to defeat. It is one of the many parts of practicing courage, sustaining effort over a long period, and engaging in internal monologues to move past through each critical stage before achieving the desired goal in the end.

How to Cultivate the Right Mindset While Decluttering

1. **Invest time in developing a**

standard for your vision and drive. Vision does not exist where it is not first seen. Go beyond your comfort zone. Immerse yourself in and savor the taste of what you desire to achieve from decluttering your life. After you have done that, go ahead and ask yourself why it means so much to you. Discover the things that excite you.

The vision you have is centered on you and your needs, and it must be entire, lucid, and brutally honest. Most often, people are ambiguous about their goals; all they have is an unclear vision of what they desire. Try to take a breather from the daily rollercoaster. Get yourself a notebook, find a serene environment, and write down the following: first is what you desire to achieve. Next is how you'll be able to track your achievements, and finally when you know that you have accomplished your goal(s).

Put everything into writing. Your mind would usually do what you will it to do. However, to reach a target, you must be clear about your mission. For this reason, begin writing your decluttering vision in complete detail.

2. Believe you'll succeed. The way we act is in keeping what we hold to be true. If you have a mindset of success, then you will be more likely to take steps that bring you closer to your target. You consider the possible options in the quest for the most promising way forward. You continue despite hindrances and challenges because you have the confidence that you will scale through and remain on the road to success.

Those who learned to develop a positive mental framework ultimately leads to a productive approach to life's challenges, while those who don't may eventually give up.

If you have the opinion that you will do well where decluttering your life is involved, then you are, in essence, instructing your brain to accomplish it. You direct your attention towards the possibilities and the key that will help you to advance. Conversely, if you believe that you can't successfully declutter your life, you train your brain to look for reasons why you cannot achieve it.

Beliefs influence how we behave. We can hold on to beliefs that move us toward our target rather than those that prevent us from achieving them.

3. Conquer one setback at a time. We tend to mentally rush to the finish line when we get attached to the outcome. In this frame of mind, we put a high demand on ourselves to succeed. We become preoccupied with all the hindrances we may be faced with, and we do not embrace progressive advancement and expansion. All we want is to fast forward to the benefits of success.

We won't successfully take care of ten challenges at a go. Our minds are not capable of choosing where to channel our awareness. Our focus becomes dispersed, and our positive energy dissolves.

We can, however, conquer one room at a time. We are capable of evaluating each room systematically from all perspectives. Finally, we can create a stratagem to declutter in a manner that has a higher possibility of yielding success.

We should devote to a method and forge ahead. Simplifying the target and focusing exclusively on the next room or aspect of our life can be accomplished. The mindset yields sustained action, which contributes to a substantial advancement over time.

4. Fortify your motivation continually. Most of the time, you are aware of precisely what you want; however, after enduring the "go-get-it" syndrome for a period, you may begin to lose drive. This stage is when you reduce your pace and likely give up. Many times, you may be required to go beyond yourself to bring out the best. Meditate on these questions: who is influenced by my dream, and who is likely to benefit from it?

Think about those you loved. In what way are they likely to be affected a year after your dream is fulfilled? How about two years afterward? You are becoming more powerful, the benefits your family and friends enjoy are starting to grow, and your influence on the society around you multiplies. Imagine how it all amasses after five years or ten years. Fixate your mind on the goal, and experience the rush of excitement that will engulf you. Go back to this visualization process every time you need to renew your inspiration.

5. Your sole competition should be you. Prototyping the mindset, stratagem, and dealings of those who have already achieved what you are chasing after is precious. By modeling, you can avoid unnecessary errors committed by other people on their way to successful decluttering. You can find out a reliable plan that hastens the advancement to your goals.

While the process of acquiring knowledge from others improves your growth, mentally contending with them results in harmful repercussions. When you compare ourselves to others, you set your sights on more successful people. This attitude causes you to feel like you are not enough and second-guess your capabilities.

When you change your standards and contend only with yourself, you move faster on your way to a productive decluttering. You will become less affected by what others are engaging in. All you are trying to do is be better than you were yesterday. You are only concerned about making your home and life adequately planned, so you should evaluate your success solely on your personal targets for decluttering.

6. Be proactive. You must be active and ready to take the bull by the horns if you want to reduce clutter. Proactivity helps you to be in charge of your life rather than sit by the sidelines, watching it get filled with junk.

If you desire success in decluttering your life, you must be capable of making difficult choices to ensure your home and life are in order. If you are proactive, then ultimately, you will be pro-growth; as a result, you have made the most crucial decision to declutter successfully.

7. Do not lose your sense of humor. Decluttering can be a turbulent and overwhelming process that leaves you worn out and exhilarated at the same time. The secret to surviving this experience while at the same time maintaining sanity lies in your ability to be humorous and able to laugh at your errors.

If you allow each obstacle to drag you down, you will be rid of your sense of drive and the ability to function. Be open to each challenge as a fundamental aspect of the process; be grateful for how it provides you with another avenue to learn without shifting your focus.

Having the proper frame of mind is an extraordinary job. You may obtain counsel and assistance, but developing the right mindset leads you to success. Only bear in mind that starting decluttering requires hard work, but the benefits are tremendous and worth the effort.

Your Quick Start Action Step:

1. Write down ten reasons why you think

you won't be able to declutter your home and life successfully.

2. Then write down at most two ways to combat each of the ten reasons listed in the first point.

3. Be ready to apply one of those two ways per problem when you begin to declutter, and the reasons in the first bullet start appearing.

Chapter 3: Planning Your Time

Chapter 3: Planning Your Time

Time organization refers to managing time optimally such that the right proportion of time is assigned to the correct activity. Effective time organization permits individuals to allocate a definite time gap to events according to their level of importance.

Even though everybody has the same 24 hours, time tends to be wasted as a result of mismanagement and lack of planning. Time organization refers to making the full use of time; after all, time is always limited.

Know which of the projects before you are most vital and the quantity of time you should assign to each. Ask yourself which work should be done first and which should be done later. This section of the book will help you deal with this challenge.

Below is detailed what makes managing your time important (in association with decluttering):

1. **Time organization helps you keep time and be disciplined.** You train yourself to work when it is necessary due to proper time

organization. To make the maximum use of time, you must write a daily task plan or a to-do list each day. Based on the order of importance and urgency to meet up with the time allotted to each task, you should then try to make a list of activities required for that day.

A to-do list will set you on track at your place of work. A person can tell what form his day will take and then work toward achieving it, thereby producing more.

2. **An effective time organization makes you a more organized person.** Putting items in their right place reduces the unnecessary time spent in search of missing files, stationery items, documents, folders, paperwork, and so on. To ensure better usage of time, people keep their workspace, booths, meeting area, conference room, or study area tidy and well arranged. Also, time management helps individuals learn how to use things properly.

3. **Proven time organization makes you more confident, as it lifts your**

morale. Due to time organization, you will be able to complete a given assignment within the time allocated for it. This benefit will cause you to be well admired in your place of work and among your colleagues.

Individuals who know the importance of time are the ones who manage to single themselves out from the crowd. People who complete work at the right time are well-liked by other people and are always the point of attraction in all places.

4. **People who stick to a time plan are the ones who understand their goals and objectives within the shortest possible period.** Making optimal use of time helps workers to meet up with goals far before the time limit and complete a task when it is necessary.

5. **Active time organization helps you reach the peak of success quickly and remain fixed at the zenith for a more extended period.** If your reason for working is merely for the sake of it, you will fail to make

an impression and will be less likely to be reckoned within your organization. Effective time organization plays a critical role in promoting a person's output. Productivity increases significantly when individuals manage their time correctly.

6. **Improved time organization helps in better planning and, ultimately, better forecasting.** People learn to organize things better and can predict where they will be in the next five years.

7. **People who complete a given task promptly are less prone to stress and anxiety.** Bear in mind that there is no sense in frittering away time only to be stressed out later on. Complete all pending tasks at the right time, and then you will have plenty of free time for your family members and acquaintances.

8. **Time organization makes it possible for a person to prioritize tasks and activities at their workplace.** It is not wise to remain foolish enough to stay overloaded. Do not be too quick to say yes to all

requests that come your way. Time organization makes it easier for a person to take on a deliberate approach in life.

How to Organize Your Time

- **Plan well**. Have a proper plan for your day before it even starts. Set up a to-do list or a task plan. Put into writing all vital tasks and activities that you need to complete in just one day with a specific amount of time assigned for each job. Assignments that take higher precedence should come at the top of the list, after which you should include those with less demanding importance. Finish following tasks one after the other; do not start a new job until after having completed older ones. Make sure also to mark the completed tasks and complete each assignment within the allotted time frame.

- **Set time limits**. Set time limits for yourself, and do everything possible to complete tasks before the stipulated time limits. Do not wait until your supervisors demand assignments from you all the time.

Endeavor to take responsibility for your work. The only person in the best position to set time limits is you. Ponder on the time you will need to dedicate to each activity and the number of days it will take. You can keep track of important dates using a planner, comparing it against the stipulated time limits.

- **Allot responsibilities**. Do not agree with every single thing that is being asked of you at your organization. Learn not to be the one doing everything. There is always someone else available to take on the tasks. You should also never consent to functions that will prove difficult to complete. Assignments should be assigned to other employees based on interests and their areas of expertise to be completed within a given time frame. People who have limited knowledge about a thing tend to require extra time to complete a task compared to someone who knows the work well.

- **Adopt the use of a day-to-day planner**. You can use a paper or digital planner, depending on your preferences. The secret to it is keeping a record of all your tasks, duties, activities, and so on. Also, you need to have an accessible way to go back to them on a day-to-day basis. Use an organizer to allow your brain a break. It is difficult to recollect everything; hence, do not sweat it.

- **Set short and long-term goals.** Embarking on tasks and activities in a company without having definite goals and objectives can be likened to a captain who has lost his way at sea. Indeed, you would be off track. Carrying out regular goal-setting can give you a definite direction concerning what you need to do to achieve specific results. To attain essential and lasting goals, recognize smaller milestone goals as you go. For instance, if you have a target that needs to be reached within six months, you might require setting more modest goals to improve on some specific skills. Your goals should be precise, determinate, attainable, significant, and time-based.

- **Manage your schedule.** Putting time

aside to finish vital assignments on your task list is essential in time organization. You may contemplate disregarding some specific time brackets on your schedule to be assured of enough time to attend to each assignment without having interruptions or other intruding conferences. You must also determine which appointments are worth visiting and those who are not. If you sense that you have little or nothing to contribute, you should not hesitate to decline such conferences. If you ever detect the need to do this, you must be civil and well-mannered about it. Be thoughtful enough to send a prior notice, most preferably, an email informing them of your absence that includes your reasons.

- **Organize tasks**. Prioritizing can be very tasking, but it gets better with time and practice. You can exercise your prioritization skills by drawing a to-do list. Tick off those activities that you need to do in a day, week, month, and so on. Putting down everything you need, whether on paper or an electronic device, will help you accomplish tasks based on their level of priority or ease of completion. If you require assistance, you might consider asking your colleague or boss (who is likely good at prioritizing tasks) how they get their work done. Having knowledge of deadlines and how each assignment affects others and the targets set by the organization can help you complete specific tasks before the rest of your colleagues. Tasks should be completed based on their level of importance.

- **Dedicate your time and energy to things you are most passionate about**. A large number of individuals try to be everything to everyone. You are likely to know someone who fits that description - or perhaps, this may even be describing you. You could offer to take part in committees at your place of work, volunteer at social gatherings, or agree to teach kids how to play basketball despite knowing that you have little time at your disposal. At one point or the other, we find ourselves in this situation. The result of such is that we become beat up, exhausted, and hateful. Devote yourself to completing a task or two at most, and decline any other offer in a civil manner.

- **Check for potential problems**. All of us waste hours going to closed stores or art centers or have missed a train due to invalid information. Your plans can even be disrupted by simple road construction. Ensure to keep your monthly itinerary up-to-date, and try to add in alternatives for specific tasks if you can see a setback coming. Check the local newspapers for reports, and always browse the internet for opening hours and train schedules.

- **Sleep at least seven hours every night**. A lack of good sleep can result in several psychological and physical problems. You must understand that it is never just about getting more done, but instead, it is about performing better.

- **Morning day routine**. The morning is a vital part of the day. A wholesome and fruitful morning will create an atmosphere for a productive day overall; hence, ensure to take morning routines seriously. Begin making plans for your morning the night before. Pick out the clothes you will wear the next day and set targets. Get up the moment your alarm goes off; do not snooze the alarm. Drink some water and practice exercises to get you revitalized. Follow your schedule strictly all through the morning, and minimize diversions to start your day off productively.

- **Select your clothes for the next day**. You do not want to spend time in the morning, deliberating on what to wear. The night before, choose an outfit for the coming day. Spread it out on a table, or hang it up in your closet. When the morning arrives, you'll be able to throw on your clothes and welcome the day quickly.

- **Set targets for the next day**. It is recommended for you to have three to four small goals daily to increase your output. Before you go to bed each night, draw a list of things you wish to accomplish the following day. By doing so, you can determine what you require from each morning and focus your attention accordingly.

- **Do not hit the snooze button**. While the few additional minutes of sleep sound tempting when you are sleepy, hitting the snooze button is never the best way to start your morning. Doing so may even make you more fatigued because you are continually disturbing your sleep pattern. When your alarm awakens you during deep and relaxing sleep, but you hit the snooze button, you revert to a lighter sleeping state. This type of sleep will not provide additional rest, and instead, it can make you more exhausted in the long run. Rather than snoozing the alarm, set the alarm to the exact time you need to get up. Do not place the alarm for 8:30 so you can have the pleasure of turning off the alarm and then getting up at 8:45. On the contrary, set the alarm for 8:45, and get up without hitting snooze.

- **Rise at least two hours early**. You want to make sure you wake up with time to spare for showering, getting dressed, eating breakfast, and doing any other important things you need to do before work or school. Make it a goal to get up about two hours before you need to be somewhere. For instance, assuming you must be at your place of work by 8:00 in the morning, get up at 6:00. This setup is subject to things like your commute; you may need to get up earlier. If it takes you an hour to commute to work, for example, you'll have to set out by 7:00 in the morning, and you will then want to aim at awaking at 5:00.

- **Eat a healthy breakfast**. You should never go without breakfast. Doing so will only leave you fatigued and sleepy all through the day. For your breakfast, avoid heavily processed foods and those with high sugar content. Consume a healthy breakfast that includes whole grains, proteins, and fruits. Opt for things like fruit and yogurt, oatmeal, and a green smoothie. Avoid pastries such as doughnuts or microwaveable breakfast foods.

- **Begin your day with exercise**. It is not until you have visited the gym that you can boost your energy. A little amount of exercise can go a long way in helping you begin the day with a lot of strength and vigor while reducing your stress levels to the bare minimum. Even a ten-minute exercise can turn the course of your day around for the better, keeping you energized all day long. You can go for a short walk around the neighborhood, practice some yoga exercises in the privacy of your room, or do a ten-minute walk on your treadmill.

- **Stay off the internet first thing in the morning.** Until you have completed everything you need to do, stay away from your phone and laptop. Set strict rules for yourself regarding when you can be on the internet. For instance, you can decide not to look at your phone until you have finished a minimum of three tasks. Social media can have very distracting effects on people. Make efforts to log out of social media platforms like Twitter and Instagram the night before. In addition to this, stay away from things like news websites. You want to avoid starting off the day with a disheartening report.

- **Plan your time carefully**. While going about your daily routine, it is crucial to keep track of time, as it is very easy to get carried away while taking a shower or eating your breakfast. To prevent this, you need to allow time for each activity and ensure that you stick to each period of time. First, though, you should make a list of all the activities you usually engage in daily and how much time you need to complete all these tasks. For instance, you may have 15 minutes to take a shower, get dressed, arrange your hair, and eat your breakfast. All you need to do is divide these activities and assign a specific amount of time to each one. While doing this, don't take your eyes off the clock to prevent yourself from spending too much time on one activity.

- **Do not multitask**. You should make it a practice to take things one step at a time as you proceed with your activities for the day. Many people think they will save more time by multitasking. However, the truth is that you will end up wasting more time and would likely be less productive at the end of the day. To be productive, complete one task at a time. That way, you will be able to channel your energy to the task at hand and complete it rather than starting multiple tasks at once and stopping midway. In addition, keep your mind off the next task on your to-do list. Although it may be challenging to keep your mind from wandering, make a concerted effort to direct your attention back to the present task.

Your Quick Start Action Step:

1. Think about the top ten activities that you waste time on in your life.

2. Write down the five most important activities of those ten imagined, and rank them from most to least severe.

3. Write down the reasons you think you waste time on them; include two reasons for each of the five.

4. Now write five ways in which organizing your time will benefit you.

Chapter 4: Organizing Family Activities

Chapter 4: Organizing Family Activities

Your daily routine could be so fixed that you hardly have time to have fun with the kids. For instance, you could be busy with work, cleaning the home, going to school, and sleeping. In order to have spare time, you will need to avoid wasting time on unnecessary activities. Also, you can look for ways to make your daily chores more interesting by turning them into games so you could include your children in your daily tasks.

Taking a closer look at your schedule, you will discover that you might still be able to find free time in your busy schedule. It is always good to spend some quality time with family. By being organized, you will be able to make some free time and reduce stress.

Why It's Important to Organize Your Family Activities

To strengthen the family bond. The primary reason for making out time for family is to ensure that you develop stronger ties with them. In most cases, kids tend to join bad groups because they feel welcomed by members of such groups, and they view them as family.

Your children need to be reassured that they are part of the family, and as such, they need to feel a sense of belonging and security. By spending quality time with them, you're indirectly telling them to always turn to you and look up to you for anything. Therefore, spending quality time with family will ensure that a deep, warm, and strong family bond is established.

To make time to talk and listen. Communication is essential to have a healthy family relationship. Spending time with your family will allow you to speak and listen to each other, thereby resolving any differences within the family.

Today, most parents often assume that taking the time to talk with their kids will be difficult, if not a waste of time, compared with talking to adults. However, parents often forget about their early days and how it felt when they were about the same age as their kids. Generally, children are often attracted to those who spend time listening to whatever they need to say. You likely may have felt the same way when you were their age.

Also, keep in mind that listening involves more than just hearing the words your child is saying while making sure you feel the message your child is trying to express. Even if it doesn't make much sense to you, it certainly does to them.

While listening to them is essential, it is also necessary to avoid jumping to conclusions, cutting them off mid-way, criticizing their ideas, or enforcing your viewpoints upon them. To show them that you're genuinely involved in the conversation, you need to suspend whatever you're doing and give them your undivided attention. Discuss a relevant subject such as sex, alcohol, or drugs directly with your kids - most notably, the teenagers. Most importantly, ensure you set a good example yourself.

To teach your children valuable lessons in life. If you fail to teach your children at home, they will be explained elsewhere. As parents, it would be disheartening if your children were to learn life's valuable lessons the hard way, such as by experiencing the pain that results from making a wrong choice.

Indeed, you can't teach your children everything, and they will learn a few lessons from their personal experiences in life. However, parents must spend time with their family to discuss some pertinent issues. Such time allows the family to put forth points or challenging conditions they are faced with and then discuss such issues as a family.

During these discussions, parents should try to seek the opinions of their children and discuss with them the matter at hand. This way, they will learn and understand how to handle various situations in life in more efficient ways.

To show affection, appreciation, and encouragement. Spending family time together allows every member of the family to show love to each other. Such displays of affection can include giving a warm hug, holding hands to pray, kind and thoughtful words of encouragement, and the giving of gifts. According to researchers, teenagers who were showed affection by being hugged, commended for a good deed, or kissed are more likely to perform better at school than those who lacked such experiences.

One good way to show affection is by asking each member of the family how they spent their day and what activities they engaged in during the day. It is often easier to criticize than to give commendations; therefore, make a conscious effort to focus on the positive qualities of each person, and tell your kids what you notice and appreciate about them. By doing so, you will be indirectly teaching them good values.

To instill family values in your children. Nowadays, it is vital to instill family values in your children to avoid being misled by the growing number of divorce cases.

As a parent, you need to set good examples for your children, because they tend to imitate your behavior and the attitude you show toward them. If you are always away from home, for instance, your children are more likely to follow that example in the future.

Thus, by spending time with your family, you will be instilling positive family values in them and building in them a sense of self-worth.

To inculcate family rituals and traditions. The little things or daily routines you perform daily or on special occasions will help create a sense of satisfaction, a sense of belonging, and inner peace within the family. Daily rituals, such as the way you greet each other, how you say goodbye on your way out, or what you say or do at mealtimes and bedtimes, can all go a long way to make the family time you spend worthwhile.

Most families that come together to celebrate special events such as wedding anniversaries, birthdays, or holidays often benefit from these gatherings, because they learn from such traditions and what happens on these occasions.

To accept the differences in each person. Family time allows each member of the family to appreciate, commend, and cherish the uniqueness in each other. By spending quality time together, you will get to know that everyone is unique in their own way. During such occasions, ensure that each family member feels excited and that everyone is shown the respect they deserve.

Avoid the mistake of forcing other members of the family to be like you or pressuring them into hiding their feelings or differences. Instead, make them feel proud of who they are.

To keep in touch with friends and relatives. The kind of society we live in today does not encourage spending time with family and interacting with friends. However, during a crisis, we can be assured that we can always turn to our family. Our children can also feel secure and happy, knowing that they have someone to turn to. Moreover, such experiences will help your children make good friends later in life.

To share the chores. During family time, you can seize the opportunity to teach your children how to be responsible by giving them specific duties or tasks while you supervise them. However, do not be too hard on them, but rather try to show a sense of humor, and remember to give commendation for a job well done.

If you spend more time with your family, gradually a special kind of relationship based on intimacy and trust will develop. This approach is necessary if you wish to have a healthy family relationship. This trust level usually becomes relevant when children are allowed to make meaningful contributions during a decision-making process.

To help you connect better with your children. The busy world out there makes most parents overlook the critical role of parenting and the part it plays in the educational life of their children. Most parents don't realize that family time offers parents the opportunity to get involved in their children's learning process.

Parents and other family members need to make time to spend together. According to research, when parents get themselves involved in the family, their children are more likely to:

- Get high test scores and grades

- Leave high school with an excellent graduating grade

- Proceed to college and attain higher education

- Develop positive attitudes and be well-behaved

Family time could involve simple activities, such as reading a story to your kids at bedtime, going through their homework with them, attending a PTA meeting, discussing your child's progress with their teachers, or any other activities that are related to their academic life. It could also involve asking your child how their day was at school, which helps if done every day.

How to Plan for Family Activities

1. Ensure your mornings work out well for you. On most mornings, we are often disorganized and tend to make mistakes during the rush. However, since if you take things easy, you can arrive at your child's school calm and still have enough energy to face the day.

2. Have a menu plan. If you don't have one already, it's advised that you start a menu plan today. Having a good menu plan help take away the daily worry of deciding what to cook for breakfast, and it will also help you stick to your budget. It is often suggested to start with a menu plan for dinners, and once you get a handle on the process, you can then begin to add breakfasts and lunches.

3. Create a family launch pad or command center. Try to have a central location where all the daily items that are needed by your family can be kept. By doing so, it will be much easier to find and use anything that is required.

4. Design a weekly visual schedule. Developing an accessible visual schedule or a calendar for each week's activities and placing them where all the members of the family can see it is an excellent way to encourage everyone to be more organized. This process will also help your kids grow into independent adults.

5. Plan for success. Reflect on the challenging tasks in your daily routine, and try to find ways of simplifying such tasks. For instance, you should think about the following things:

- Selecting your child's school uniforms first thing in the morning or the night before.

- Having a box for hair accessories where everything needed is kept together, such as a hairbrush, hair spray, and hair ties.

- Keeping a homework box where everything you need for your child's homework is stored for easy access.

- Keeping your daughter's dance bags in the last drawer of your central launchpad so that everything she needs is held together and ready for dance class afternoons.

6. Design a cleaning routine. Everyone must decide when to clean, how to clean, and how often to clean the house. The most important thing is having a routine that works well for you and sticking to it. When you find a routine, and you consistently stay on track, it can help you minimize the stress of cleaning chores.

7. Get your children involved in cleaning and household chores. Parents often feel that involving their children in cooking, cleaning, washing, and other household chores is an extra chore on its own. After all, it will take a longer time to teach them, yet the results are not guaranteed. In the end, it would be as good as doing it yourself but with extra stress. However, such activities will help teach your child essential life skills and give them a higher sense of self-worth, fulfillment, and independence.

8. Create a chore chart. Utilizing a regular schedule of chores for your children will help them develop a sense of responsibility. There are various ways to monitor these chores and add an incentive or compensation to each completed task, such as pocket money.

9. Have a personal to-do list. By nature, I'm a very religious list-maker, but I have this bad habit of scribbling on any paper scrap, which eventually gets misplaced. But now, I'm making a more conscious effort to have an organized to-do list that will help sort out tasks according to category. It will also keep everything together in one place. Besides, it helps me to prioritize all my tasks.

To make your weekly to-do list more easily accessible, you can print it out such that you can always sort out family-related and work-related tasks while on the move.

10. Prioritize the most important things to your family. What matters in one family differs from others. Therefore, each family must determine what matters the most to them. Then prioritize those organizational tools that are likely to be most useful in the home. How you want your children to view your home after they grow up and live on their own is a good starting point for you to review your priorities.

11. Identify time wasters. By detecting and eliminating time-wasting activities, you can create extra time for you and your family. To identify such events, you may need to sit down and discuss the issue as a team.

12. Prepare for family outings. Ensure that you make plans for pleasurable family outings and ones that every member of the family will enjoy. These plans can be done by choosing activities that everyone, including your children, can participate in and be excited about. If you observe that your teenage child doesn't seem to be excited about group outings, you can rekindle his or her interest by allowing him or her to choose the activities for the outing.

13. Make good use of Saturdays. If your work permits to rest on Saturdays, you can make good use of that day for family-related activities. You could spend the day riding bicycles with the kids or eating ice cream. Another suggestion is to go on a day visit to a nearby tourist attraction center. Such outings will help your children get out of the house, and they will also learn more about their community. Other Saturday activities could include:

- Spending some time outdoors at the closest national park or beach

- A visit to a fire station to learn what it takes to be a fireman

- Visiting a science or an art museum

- Participating in volunteer work together with your kids

14. Find a family hobby. Finding something interesting that everyone will like doing is a great way to spend some quality time together weekly. For instance, you can spend time with your kids while teaching them a new skill. Such activities include:

- Teaching your children how to build a simple game (if your son or daughter loves playing video games)

- Teaching them how to cook (if your son or daughter loves cooking)

- Joining a robotics club together (if they like playing with electronics)

Your Quick Start Action Step:

1. Ask your partner if he or she is happy with the amount of time you spend with them daily. If your partner isn't around, ask any of your children around you at the time.

2. Ask them how and where they want you to improve concerning family time.

3. Now, write down the specific family activities you want to engage them in for the next month.

Chapter 5: Achieving a Clutter-Free Home

Chapter 5: Achieving a Clutter-Free Home

Many people love the idea of living a simple, uncluttered life; a life with less stress, less to organize, less debt, less to clean, and more money and energy to pursue their passions. They have considered getting rid of unnecessary possessions and are ready to declutter. However, many people don't know where they should start.

After so much brainstorming, many still feel anxious and confused when it comes to decluttering their homes. But the good news is that the process of decluttering shouldn't be as painful as some make it appear. Various experiences demonstrate that decluttering can be a lot of fun.

However, as fun as it can be, decluttering can also be challenging. Whether you decide to declutter by using downsizing efforts or by simplifying your life, both require effort and sacrifice. It is often suggested that you tackle the entire process in stages. For example, you can start by taking on a room, space, or a small zone within a place such as your laundry cabinets. Once you've completed the present task, you can then move on to the next room or space. The success you experience from such smaller tasks will boost your confidence, and you will be ready for more significant jobs.

Note that a decluttered home = a decluttered life; therefore, ensure that you solve every clutter need.

You might find it surprising to know that you don't need sophisticated tools to declutter your home. Sometimes all you need is three baskets or bins tagged for five different purposes. These include the following:

- **The put-away bin:** These are items that are found where they aren't supposed to be that need to be returned to their designated spots. Examples are a teacup in the bathroom or a pair of socks in the kitchen.

- **The recycle bin:** This bin contains items that could be recycled, such as plastic bags, glass, and paper.

- **Mend/fix bin:** This bin includes items that need to be cleaned or repaired, such as your favorite pair of shoes.

- **Trash bin:** Items that are irredeemable are kept in this designated bin and can be emptied into the family trash immediately for disposal.

- **Donate bin:** This bin is meant for items that you no longer need, but that can be useful to others, such as a charitable organization or other individuals.

If these bins are not available, you can make use of cardboard boxes as well. The containers can be kept in a central location in your home; you can keep them in each room as you declutter. One important thing to avoid is searching for containers in the middle of a decluttering process; it's best to set up the bins before you commence.

Why a Clutter-Free Home Is Important

There are a couple of benefits you will derive from taking time to declutter your home. Some of these benefits are highlighted below:

- **Financial:** We could be coerced into buying duplicates of items we already own if we are not cautious. Clutter costs lots of money, especially when we can't find things that we know we possess.

- **Time:** Owning so many possessions consumes more time than we could ever imagine. When every item is in its right place, we can save nearly an hour per day. You could then use this amount of time for yourself and your family.

- **Space:** Decluttering your home means that you will have more space for playing, living, and working. Clutter-free spaces are more attractive and can be used for greater purposes.

- **Emotional:** When we declutter our life, we can live a more balanced, peaceful, and energy-filled life. Such a healthy way of living will improve our health, make us happy, and reduce anxiety.

- **Find stuff:** When we declutter our home, it will help reduce the time that would have wasted searching for stuff.

How to Declutter Your Home

Bathrooms. You can start with your medicine cabinet in the bathroom. Firstly, bring everything out and dispose of expired medications, lotions, and other skincare products. Whatever you still wish to keep should be returned to the cabinet without delays. Keep the items you regularly use at eye level.

You can then proceed to any other cabinet drawers. As done before, take everything out of the drawer, and carry out a fast evaluation of what item(s) you wish to keep and those that need to be disposed of. Once you're done sorting that out, return the items you want to keep into the drawers, with the things most important stored in the first drawers.

At this point, repeat the same exercise with your tub/shower. Lastly, remove whatever item you find below your bathroom sink and declutter such items.

Every stray item would eventually be sorted out into any of the five baskets/bins you've already labeled according to their purpose.

Bedrooms. The first thing you need to do is make your bed. If the bed is unmade, it will be difficult to notice any progress while decluttering a room.

You can then proceed to remove all the clothes on the nightstands, along with any other item that doesn't belong there, and put them in one of the tagged bins. Other items include an already completed book, a broken eyeglass, or a dried-up pen.

You should also do the same with the tops of your chests and dressers. Take your time searching for any clothing that is hanging randomly after putting each item in its place. Any cloth that needs to be folded or hung should go into the put-away bin.

Make sure to go through each drawer carefully. Pull everything out, search for clothes that you no longer wear, and transfer them into the donation bin. Fold the rest and arrange them back into the drawer.

If you have a vanity table or a desk in your bedroom, this should be the next thing you tackle. Avoid the temptation to shove items back into drawers, and instead, place them in your put-away bin or recycle bin, especially items you haven't used for the past six months. Fold or hang and store any clothing you still need, and keep them in their proper places.

Closet and clothing. The best way to declutter your closet is to declutter all your clothing by type first. This technique means that you start with your dresses, then denim, shoes, and boots.

This method makes it easier to decide what items to keep and which things need to be tossed away. For instance, if you focus on your denim collection at once, you will see that deciding which pair of jeans to keep or discard will be easier. This approach also saves time compared with trying to sort out all the clothes in your closet at once.

After sorting out all the type of clothing, you're likely to have four piles to tackle:

> 1. Discard any item that was randomly abandoned at the wrong spot. For example, if you found a tie in your closet, you can put it back in your dresser.

> 2. All dirty laundry should be kept in the hamper or transferred to the laundry room.

3. All worn-out clothes that need cleaning or mending should be packed and sent to the dry cleaner or tailor accordingly.

4. All items that you have no use for should go into the donation bin and dropped off at a consignment store or donation center.

Entryways, foyers, and mudrooms. Although you may not have a mudroom or foyer in your home, you most certainly have an entryway that leads into the house. Regardless of the size, you need to declutter it regularly to make the entryway functional.

If there is any console, tables, or desk in your entryway, this might be the best place to start from. Just as you did for your closet, go through each drawer, and empty all the contents in it. Now, decide which items need to be tossed or kept. As much as you can, decongest the top drawer to make enough space for your keys and other essential items.

Kitchen. Due to the many different activities that take place in the kitchen, keeping it clutter-free can be challenging. Because of activities such as- cooking, eating, and socializing, various types of items are held in the kitchen. In this instance, as well, you should focus on one group of items at a time. For example, you may decide to declutter the glassware, bakeware, or cutting boards.

You may begin by completely emptying the top cabinet, selecting items that are still needed, and tossing those you no longer need. You can then return the useful items to their proper places. Next, focus on the lower cabinets and the space below your kitchen sink.

The countertops should not be left out. Decongest the countertops as much as possible by moving items that litter the countertops, and keep them in the appropriate storage spaces. Only items that you use daily should be kept on the countertops.

The last thing you need to do is to return anything that doesn't belong in the kitchen back to their rightful storage spaces.

Living room. Aside from the kitchen, the living room is yet another problematic place to declutter. The reason is because of the vital functions of this room. Usually, the living room doesn't have ample storage spaces. It is often suggested that:

- Items that are used regularly have permanent storage space. Such items include magazines, books, and remote controls.

- You also declutter this space regularly.

You can begin with the console, side tables, and bookcases. Next, you can focus on your coffee table and entertainment area. Just as in previous cases, empty all the items in the store and decide what object needs to be returned to its proper storage spaces and those that need to be tossed.

Now, you can shift your focus to electronics. Any gadgets not directly connected to your home theater system or television should be removed. Then ask yourself if you still use it or if it still works. Items such as gaming equipment, chargers, and other gadgets should be kept in their designated places.

Finally, focus on the toys. Examine each toy to sort out those that are damaged. Again, ask yourself if it's still functional and whether your kid still plays with it. Finding an answer to these questions will determine whether you should store or recycle each toy.

Your Quick Start Action Step:

1. Make a mental picture of the level of disorganization in every room in your house, including your bathroom and kitchen.

2. Envision how you want those rooms to look after organizing them.

3. Now, write down the rooms you want to declutter, from the easiest to the most difficult, and how long it will take you to finish each one.

4. To learn more about decluttering your home, check out the book from the author entitled "Declutter your Home: Simple Step-by-Step Decluttering Strategies on How to Declutter and Organize to De-Stress and Simplify your Life" in the online store.

Chapter 6: Organizing Your Finances

Chapter 6: Organizing Your Finances

Decluttering your home will make it look cozy and neat. The interesting thing to note is that all it takes is the simple process of deciding what items are no longer necessary and should be discarded immediately. Discarding certain items may be a tough choice to make; however, we usually know what items we still need and those we don't.

This situation is not the case when it comes to decluttering your financial life, though. The entire process involved is difficult to understand and even more challenging to apply. What makes physical decluttering comparatively easier is that items you no longer need are easier to notice, like the unused dumbbell in your bedroom that hits your toe at least twice a day. With physical objects, you'll often be reminded that they need to be tossed. On the contrary, cluttered money is not as visible.

It might interest you to know that the same principles that will help a newbie declutter his or her financial life are also applicable to minimalists.

In the financial world, messy finances usually lead to worry and anxiety. One of the best decisions you can ever make is to decide to simplify your economic life. To oversee your spending, you may need to cut down on your bills, expense, and purchases.

Why It Is Necessary to Organize Your Finances

Organizing your finances will help you see clearly how to allocate your money the best and then provide ideas on what items to purchase based on your financial status. It will protect you against the pain that comes with overspending and being in so much debt. Many feel that budgeting prevents them from enjoying their lives; however, what it does is ensures that you enjoy stuff within your financial limitations.

Although it requires a lot of calculations and brainstorming, it will pay off in the end. Additionally, it comes with a lot of life-enhancing benefits, such as those highlighted below:

- **You gain control over your money**: You will be cautious about how you save and spend your money, and it will help you avoid the stress of suddenly adjusting to a lack of funds because you failed to plan how to spend your money initially. Budgeting also offers you the opportunity to decide whether you want to sacrifice long-term benefits for short-term spending.

- **Help you focus on your money goals:** Unnecessary spending can be avoided if you properly plan how you should spend your money. Any item or service that will not help you achieve your financial goals can easily be avoided.

- **It makes you conscious of what is going on with your money:** You know exactly how much you're expecting, how soon it will be spent, and what you will spend it on. Being financially organized will save you from wondering where your money went at the end of every month. Also, you will be able to figure out how much you're worth financially and what you can afford to buy, save, and invest.

You will also be able to cut down on your debts.

- **Helps you organize your spending and savings better:** When you consciously divide your money into different categories of savings and expenditures, you will be able to monitor your spending and know exactly how much spending is required on each. With that, it will be much easier to adjust when necessary. Such an organization can also be used for reference purposes in filing your financial statements, receipts, and bills. In addition, your financial transactions can be presented at tax time or for creditor questions and will help you save some energy and time as well.

- **You will be able to save for expected and unexpected costs:** By being organized, you will be able to plan and set some money aside for unforeseen expenses.

- **Helps you to discuss financial matters with your family:** Automation can assist you in quickly considering how money is being spent with them especially if the funds will be significantly shared with your partner or other members of the family. This method will foster teamwork, help you pursue common financial goals, and help to avoid financial conflicts revolving around how money was spent.

- **Helps you to produce extra money:** It will make it easier for you to avoid unnecessary spending, penalties for late fees, and incurred interests.

How to Plan Your Finances

Step 1: Define specific financial goals (with actual figures). Many people often suggest that you can begin decluttering your finances by clearing all outstanding bills and financial obligations first to determine your financial standing. Although this is a crucial step, it shouldn't be your starting point.

First, you need to be clear about your financial goals, or it will be difficult for you to organize your finances logically.

Your financial goal shouldn't be an arbitrary one, such as saving up to four months' worth of living expenses in an emergency account. That translates to nothing meaningful if there is no actual figure to relate with.

It is, however, more meaningful if you put it this way: "I want to save $7,000 in an emergency account by the end of 2019." This statement is much better than saying the following: "I want to open an emergency account."

Once you're done with the numbers, you can then proceed to the next step by developing habits and financial behaviors that will assist you in achieving your goal.

Step 2: Know where you stand. The next step is to determine your financial standing. At this point, you may need to gather all your financial documents such as your credit card statements, bank statements, loan papers, bills, mortgage papers, and insurance documents. All of these will help you get a clear picture of your financial worth, how much money you are expecting, and how much you plan to spend monthly.

You may be wondering why such an evaluation is necessary. Author Kate Northrup, in her bestselling book "Money: A Love Story", said that most people couldn't account for how much they earned and how much they've spent within the $100 range, all within the previous month.

It can be difficult, if not impossible, to declutter if you can't properly account for your financial status. Most individuals, especially those in debt, try as much as possible to avoid going through this part, as they fear numbers. However, if you really want to get your financial situation together, you must decide where you want to be (Step 1), but you can't get to where you want to be without knowing where you presently stand financially.

Below are some suggestions for what to watch out for, while going through your financial documents:

- How much money do you earn as a monthly salary?

- How much extra money do you earn each month from investments or side hustles?

- How much money do you owe?

- What kinds of debts do you have? What are the interest rates? How much do you pay back monthly?

- How much money are you saving for retirement, and is it enough?

- How much do you have in your emergency savings account?

Only a few areas have been discussed above for you to think about before you continue with your investigation. However, you can also look for other loopholes to investigate.

Some miscellaneous non-monthly expenses usually catch people off guard. These include costs such as medical bills, money spent on Christmas shopping, dental fees, annual fees, and web hosting expenses.

Step 3: Figure out where you're leaking money. If the whole process of decluttering your finances is new to you, then you may lose money. This money can be lost in different ways, such as:

- Buying unnecessary products or services
- Buying at very high prices
- Payment of fees or bills

At this point, you must look at how you spend and take specific steps to regulate your spending where necessary. When you reduce the amount of money you waste, you will be able to manage your financial affairs without difficulties.

Here is where beginners can begin looking for leaks:

- Do you purchase additional products or services? In other words, do you buy things you do not need? These products or services could include cable subscriptions, movie tickets, and a lot more. Do you purchase products at very high rates?

- Are there possibilities for reducing your bills? For example, you can search for a cheaper insurance premium.

Here is where you can look after having the basics covered:

- Is there any way you can reduce the fees on some of your accounts if not all? You can search for an online bank that operates without fees or tries bargaining for a lower annual percentage rate (APR).

Since the goal is not only to save money, people are advised to use different ways to make extra cash. These include things such as selling old properties or by starting up a side business outside of their regular jobs.

Step 4: After figuring out where your money is leaking from, the next thing to do is to go paperless. This method means transferring all your financial files to a cloud system. This approach will help you access all your financial details without the difficulties that come with bulky paper files. You can easily search for whichever file you need on the cloud system.

The paper files are scanned, well arranged, and then uploaded to a safe cloud system. New financial details should be uploaded at least once a month. The only part of this step that takes a lot of time is when you have to scan all the paper files you've had for years and manually transfer them to a cloud system. After this step is completed, you can relax and stop worrying about a stack of paper files.

Another advantage of transferring all your paper files to a cloud networking service is that you can keep a record for everything going on in your financial life with the help of tools like Mint.com and other similar services. Mint.com can be used to set up budgets and goals and review fees and investments.

Step 5: Automate as much as you can. In a bid to be in control of your budget, you may need to automate it as much as you can. Carl Richard, the author of "The One-page Financial Plan", explains in his book that those who have thoughts of saving may end up not saving at all.

In decluttering your finances, below are a couple of the areas where you can automate your money:

- **Savings**: In decluttering your finances, you must automate your savings. You can set up an automatic saving plan in which money is transferred to your savings account from your checking account. For instance, a certain amount, such as $500, is transferred to a particular account for emergency purposes at least once every month.

- **Retirement and investments**: You can go to the HR department at work to set up the automatic deposit of your paycheck. The process of doing this is straightforward, and apart from losing extra cash, you have absolutely nothing to lose. Also, if you have an IRA (individual retirement account), you can create an automatic deposit into an account of your choice.

Step 6: Avoid being in debt. This step can seem challenging to do, but it is achievable. There is great satisfaction in paying in full for what you buy without having to be indebted to anyone.

So, how do you get rid of your debt? First, save up to $1,000 to fund your emergencies. After doing this, make a list of all the money you owe, and then start paying off the debt one after the other, from the lowest amount to the highest.

Once the lowest debt is cleared, add the amount you paid to the next smallest debt to keep the ball rolling until all your debts are removed. This process is known as the debt snowball.

Step 7: Do you need help with your financial life? Don't be too shy or proud to get one. Put yourself in order before inviting a helper.

You could hire a personal financial accountant, or you could opt for counseling, especially in areas you are having problems with. You don't have to do both at once, but make sure you get help whenever you need one.

A financial accountant could help you with your taxes, while counseling could help solve financial problems like debt, overspending, and a lot more.

Your Quick Start Action Step:

1. Make a mental note of your needs and your wants.

2. Go through your bank statements, and highlight irrelevant things you have spent money on.

3. Now, write down your budget for the next month and your financial goals (or target) for the next three months.

To learn more about financial success and solving debt problems, check out "Minimalist Budget: Simple and Practical Budgeting Strategies to Save Money, Avoid Compulsive Spending, Pay Off Debt and Simplify Your Life" by Marie S. Davenport in the online store.

Chapter 7: Decluttering with Others in Your Life

Chapter 7: Decluttering with Others in Your Life

Some of us have been in a relationship with someone who we thought was the one, and we've experienced one thing: inconsistency. During the first few months of a relationship, your partner seems perfect, does everything right, and treats you well - then, they stop.

In times like this, decluttering your relationship is what you should do. Decluttering with others is a process that means avoiding people who become toxic to your life and affect your happiness. Your emotional and mental health should be your highest priority; therefore, learn to let go of people who impact your health negatively.

Leaving a relationship can be painful, no matter how toxic or offensive it is. We find it very difficult to let go of friends, family members, spouses, and business partners who don't value us or limit us. The reason is because of the effort, time, and resources we've put into building such relationships. Often, the ones who are so dear to us and who we have known for many years cause the most considerable pain.

The pain can reach a point where you would choose to make the hard decision of getting rid of them instead of sticking around and enduring the pain. However, in some cases, the drowning thoughts, worry, and depression are due to the individual's inability to manage relationships. You are in control of your feelings, and how you choose to respond to any situation is a matter of choice. The moment you understand this theory is the moment you will be able to live a quiet life that is free of aches.

This chapter will talk about specific issues you may likely encounter in your relationship with people. It will also help to build up and improve your communication skills. It will also talk about unhealthy relationships and how to handle them.

Why It's Important to Declutter with Others in Your Life

1. You waste a lot of energy dealing with toxic people: You must stop remaining in unhealthy relationships. Stop talking to toxic people; you don't owe anyone an explanation for making such a decision except those you were close to. You can open up to them; it is not uncommon for friends or even family members to drift apart. It is your responsibility to protect your happiness and live a peaceful life. Therefore, no matter how long you've been friends with a person, once you realize that the relationship is toxic, cut them off. Being with toxic people is a massive waste of time and energy.

2. You'll have more time for yourself: Having quality time with yourself is very refreshing. When you declutter your relationship with others, it gives you time to have a better relationship with yourself. If you want to lead a more purposeful life, then allow more time to relate with yourself. There are many ways you can do to fill up the empty space you feel inside. You could revive the inner you, forgive yourself, and learn to love yourself, but the best way is by creating more time for yourself alone to reflect on things. Having toxic people around could hinder your alone time and further drown you with problems.

3. Being criticized continuously is exhausting: Constant criticism is not healthy as it negatively affects your mentality and results. Being criticized continually can make you doubt your worth. You may begin to lose control of yourself, always looking for others' approval and living below your standards, and adopting another's. Keeping people who judge you still is bad for you, therefore cut them off. You don't have to live your life based on someone else's judgment. Stay away from friends, family members, and other people who do not know your true worth and do not love and accept you for who you are.

4. You'll reach your goals sooner: Toxic people around you can delay you from reaching your goals. They take attention away from your goals. Once you begin to stay away from them, you'll get back on course.

5. You'll dedicate more time to the people that matter. Not all your friends are toxic; there are most likely some who are genuine, and you should keep them. You can do this by spending more time with these people. Having new friends and talking with them can be very interesting, but they shouldn't take up all your time and effort. Disconnecting from those who don't add value to your life gives you enough time to strengthen your relationships with real friends. Aside from that, you also get to spend time with yourself.

How to Declutter with Others

You need to learn to love and hold yourself at very high esteem. With this, you won't condone any destructive relationship for any reason. The following are things you need to know about decluttering relationships:

- **Stop judging people around you:** You cannot get rid of people who do not care about you or respect you when you are doing the same thing to others. Stop judging people, and instead, care for them and value them for who they are. You are not in a position to change anybody, and so you shouldn't even attempt to do so. Accept people for who they are and not for who you want them to be. Lower your expectations of people if they are too high; we are all looking for someone who will love and value us for who we are. So, why set an unrealistic standard that no one can meet? Think deep before you cut anyone off; you could lose a diamond in search of glitter.

- **Stay away from people who make you unhappy:** Emotions or feelings can be contagious. Remain around happy people, and you will tend to become happy, but stay around unhappy people, and the reverse is the case. Some people are fond of complaining about everything, and they never seem to be satisfied with life. When you are always around such people, their misery can be transferred to you. Others tend to make you sad with their judgments and complain about your life - some of them do this without even knowing. The best thing you can do for yourself is to avoid them and have peace of mind.

- **Reduce your relationship with family members who affect you emotionally.** When it comes to family members, you cannot get rid of them, for they are a part of your existence. However, you can reduce your relationship with them. Set a boundary between you and that family member you love so much and can't completely cut off. This family member could be your favorite sibling, your best uncle or aunt, or even a parent who keeps nagging about your life, makes you feel unworthy of love and keeps opening up old wounds and makes life miserable. Since it is your responsibility to guard your heart, then there is no crime in avoiding those who keep hurting you. They are your family members, and yes, you love them, and you know they love you too and want the best for you, but this should not be done at the expense of your happiness.

- **Surround yourself with happy people:** The primary aim of decluttering your relationships with others is to have peace of mind and happiness. Therefore, happiness is a commodity sought after by all, including you. If you are looking for happiness, find happy people. Happy people always give you a reason to smile; they are always full of life, and you should surround yourself with them.

- **Surround yourself with positive people:** Positive people are not complainers; they find the good in everybody and every condition. These are the kind of people you should have around you. One way to find happiness is to be thankful for every little thing you have.

- **Find people with the same mindset and interests:** Staying around people who share common interests with you can be very inspiring. In your relationship with these people, you're not just on the receiving end, but you can also add value to their lives since you are interested in the same things. You can never feel alone when you are with them.

- **Surround yourself with successful people:** Earlier, we talked about happiness being contagious, but so is a success. The people you hang out with determining who you are or who you will be. When you begin to stay around people who have achieved great things, you gradually start to think, talk, and act like them. Soon, you will accomplish great things as well.

- **Be a good friend:** The people you are cutting off are described as harmful or toxic friends. It is hypocrisy to be cutting off people who do the exact things you do to others. Do you ever pay attention to the feelings of others? Do you constantly nag about other people's lives? Be a good friend if you need a good friend.

Letting Go of Negative People

This step is a tough decision to make. We find it hard to let go of the people we have loved. Maybe because of the time and energy we've invested for so many years to keep the relationship going. However, this step is essential to have the peace of mind you long for.

Below are some tips on how to get out of a destructive relationship:

- **Consider the positives of life without this person**: Sometimes, all we need do is think. Think about all the exciting and positive things you could do without this friend or partner in your life like the things you want to do, but you are restricted because of this person. Think about the positive turn your life would take if the relationship is ended. Your emotions could hinder your decision, so try hard to think with your head and not your heart.

- **Consider the fallout of saying goodbye**: You must take time to reflect on the consequences of saying goodbye. Ending a relationship with one person could affect your relationship with others. Are you ready to lose anyone attached to you through this person? Are you strong enough to handle the heartbreak? How would the person react to this decision? These are some of the things you should reflect upon. Sit back and think about all the possible reactions of the person and how you would handle them. Take time to assess the after-effects of ending the relationship or of staying in it, and then you should choose.

- **Define what goodbye means**: For a relationship, define what goodbye means to you. Some relationships end with no form of communication at all, while others involve people still talking to one another at times with precaution. So how do you want yours to go?

As explained earlier, you can't completely get rid of family members, because they are part of your existence, whether you like it or not. So, in cases like these, setting boundaries could be the best way out. For other people, you can either cut them off entirely or relate with them differently. In other words, you can decide how and when to talk to them, how they affect your emotional health, and what to condone from them. However, this time, you shouldn't allow them to hurt you, as you are in control.

- **Communicate your intention without blame**: Despite the pain these people have caused you, ending the relationship without any form of explanation isn't the right way to go about it. A simple statement to back up your decision will do. You can call this person, send them a letter, or meet up with them; either way, give them a reason. You don't have to blame anyone for your decision or concentrate on the person's imperfections.

- **Create a plan for a negative reaction**: Have a backup plan for any negative reactions in the future. You can discuss your decision with people who knew about your relationship with the individual, telling them about your reason for ending it without tarnishing the image of the person. So, in case of a bad or stressful situation, they will support you.

- **Accept that it can be a process**: Moving on from a relationship can take a while. For some, it can take years, while for others, it can take months. Whatever the case is, know that letting go is a process. Frequently, it can be so hard that some people try to build up the relationship again, only to worsen the situation. Acknowledge that moving on can take time, and you will be able to stand on your own eventually.

- **Allow yourself to grieve**: When you let go of someone that was close or dear to you, it is not unusual to grieve over them. You feel the pain, and the loss and your heart might ache, but do not discard it, for this is part of the healing process. When you allow yourself to grieve, the pain leaves sooner than you expect, and you can start all over again.

Your Quick Start Action Step:

1. Make a table of three columns. List names of people who have contributed positively to your life in the left column, a list of people who haven't added anything to your life in the middle column, and people who have contributed negatively to your life on the right.

2. Make another table of three columns. This time, make a list of people to whom you've contributed something on the left, people you've contributed nothing to their life in the middle, and people you have contributed negatively to their life on the right.

3. Write specific goals for how you intend to contribute positively to people around you.

Now write down a list of people you intend to cut from your life gradually.

Chapter 8: Freeing Your Mind from Worry, Anxiety, and Stress

Chapter 8: Freeing Your Mind from Worry, Anxiety, and Stress

For a significant part of our lives, we all struggle with mental clutter. We always feel like whatever happens; mental clutter is always present; something is continually running through our mind. It could be a new thing that is making us feel worried or disorganized; it might be a memory haunting us. Some days, it might be bearable, and other days, it might not. However, the feeling is always present.

The voices you hear in your head will never be still: You keep hearing your boss instructing you to get the reports ready by Friday, your son telling you not to forget about soccer practice on Saturday, or the voices of your parents reminding you to help them clean up the house this weekend.

We all have places to be every day, including the strenuous jobs we do daily at home or work. It might feel too intense, and turbulent thoughts may disturb our minds. A few of us may even hear voices echoing from past experiences.

Causes of Mental Clutter

Daily stress. The main reason a lot of people feel like life is overwhelming is that they are extremely stressed. The stress caused by physical clutter, information overload, and the limitless options needed for these things can set off a few mental health problems, such as depression, generalized anxiety, and panic attacks.

Add all these to the real concerns and worries in your life, and you might start to experience muscle pain, chest pain, sleep problems, intestinal disorders, frequent infections, headaches, and stomach disorders. This finding is according to the American Psychological Association and several studies that prove a link between physical problems and stress.

The moment life starts to become complicated and overwhelming. Our subconscious mind begins to seek escape options. Excess harmful exposure, an abundance of options, and excess input are likely to set off an unhealthy coping mechanism.

The paradox of choice. Concerning mental health, the freedom of choice (which is honored in free societies) may have a diminishing effect. The phrase "paradox of choice" was created by Barry

Schwartz, a psychologist. According to Schwartz, when choices are abundant, it results in more paralysis, anxiety, dissatisfaction, and confusion. Additional decisions might result in better outcomes without necessarily making you happy.

Jeans are very popular. Try to buy a pair, and you will have to choose from several options that are available: skinny, vintage wash, baggy fit, button fly, boot cut, or wide leg. The thought of shopping is enough to stress you out.

Too much stuff. Most of our houses are packed with clothes that may never be worn, books that will never be read, gadgets that are never used, or toys that have never been touched. Then there are many unread messages on our computers, our phones keep giving us notifications like "insufficient storage space", and our desktop area is filled with clutter.

A reply must be sent to every text and email. The newest device or gadget must be bought. Everything seems serious and vital.

These demands make us always busy, occupied with irrelevant things, suppressing our emotions, and getting emotionless toward the people around us.

Often, we feel like decluttering is too time-consuming, and we would instead study new things and information. Eventually, all these activities will result in emotional and mental stress. While processing all the things we experience, we ruminate, we assess and get incredibly anxious.

The negativity bias. This bias refers to our inclination to respond to negative stimuli more strongly compared to positive stimuli. The neural activity produced by negative stimuli is higher compared to that created by positive stimuli of equal magnitude (in terms of sound and light). The brain also senses negative stimuli faster and easier than positive ones. "The brain is similar to Velcro for the negative experience; whereas, for positive experiences, it can be likened to Teflon." - Hanson.

Thus, how do negative stimuli affect your thoughts? It indicates that you are inclined to worry, overthink, and evaluate situations more negatively. You view challenges as particularly tricky and threats as extra threatening. There is a feeling of realness for every negative thought that filters into your mind, so you instantly accept it as reality. However, you do not live in a cave, going through near-death experiences every day. Although you might be inclined to view things negatively, you can choose to avoid accepting that inclination.

Meditation

Meditation is an age-old tradition that is believed to have originated in Hindu, Chinese, and Buddhist cultures. There are so many methods of practicing meditation, but a majority of these methods start with the same steps: Sitting peacefully, concentrating all your attention on breathing, and discarding all distractions.

The objective of meditation differs in the kind of medication practice and the desired result of the participant. However, for the purpose of this book, we recommend meditation as a kind of mind-training tool that also helps you control your thoughts; regardless of whether you are in the sitting position or not during meditation.

The positive effects of meditation eventually start to become evident in your daily life, helping you to stop over-thinking, controlling worry and resulting in a lot of health benefits, which you will discover as you read on.

The secret to having a positive outcome with meditation is to keep practicing.

By dedicating a part of your day to meditation, you will develop your skills and experience the eventual benefits on your emotional, mental, and physical health.

Let us start with the basic 10-minute meditation that you can start right now. It is uncomplicated and straightforward. It does not require any special equipment or clothing. The only thing you need is a quiet place and the dedication to follow through.

This type of meditation is a fundamental but effective 11-part process that can be used to develop the habit.

1. Choose a serene, peaceful environment for your meditation. Practice where the door can be shut, and you can be completely alone.

2. Choose a specific time of the day for your session. If you have started a deep breathing session, this can be used as an

activator (and starting point) for your new meditation practice. You can also select another activator and meditate at a different time of the day.

3. Decide if you want to meditate by sitting on a pillow, a sofa, a chair or on the floor. Since you might fall asleep, try not to lean backward.

4. Get rid of every distraction, and switch off every digital gadget or other gadgets that may be noisy. Take your pet out of the room.

5. Fix a timer for 10 minutes.

6. Sit cross-legged or normally sit, either on a chair or a cushion placed on the floor. Maintain an erect spine, and place your hands softly over your lap.

7. Keep your eyes closed. But if you prefer to open them, do it while looking downward. Then inhale a few deep cleansing breaths using your nose. We advise taking three or four breaths at once.

8. Slowly become aware of your breathing. Take note of the air going in and out of your nostrils and the upward and downward movements of your abdomen. Do not force your breaths, but rather let them come spontaneously.

9. Concentrate on your breathing. You can also try to mentally picture the word "in" while you inhale and "out" while exhaling.

10. In the initial stages, you would be distracted by your thoughts. Each time you are distracted, let go of those thoughts gently and focus your attention back to the process of breathing.

11. Do not beat yourself up over distracting thoughts. Your monkey mind is merely trying to take control. Guide your mind back to concentrating all the attention on breathing. You might have to do this a few times in the beginning.

12. While all your concentration is on your breathing, you will likely be more aware of

other sensations and perceptions, such as physical unease, emotions, or sounds. Just take note of the times you become aware of them and carefully focus your attention back to the sensational breathing.

Your aim is to progressively become aware of all sensations, thoughts, feelings, and emotions as they develop and fade away. Look at them as if you are only viewing them from a distance with no internal comments or judgment.

Instead of your mind taking charge and losing focus as soon as a distraction or thought occurs, eventually, you can control your mind at a maximum level and become skilled at redirecting focus back to where you are at that moment.

Initially, you might feel as if you are in a constant fight with your monkey mind. However, consistent practice means that there will be no need to redirect your thoughts always. Naturally, thoughts begin to fade away, and your brain becomes open to the limitless vastness and silence of merely being there. This moment is an intensely quiet and satisfying feeling.

Mindfulness

Gradual, deep, rhythmic breathing is one effective method of isolating negative thoughts and controlling your mind. This concentrated breathing activates the parasympathetic nervous system, causing muscle relaxation, a reduction in heart rate, normalized brain activity, and a quiet mind.

Deep breathing creates a connection between you and your body, taking your awareness away from your anxiety and silencing the internal conversations in your brain. Deep breathing results in physiological changes that are commonly called the "relaxation response".

If you practice a few minutes of abdominal breathing daily, you are developing a permanent habit that has been discovered to lower stress, clear your mind, and enhance the relaxation of the body and mind. This relaxation technique is based on many years of extensive research and testing. Try out the following steps:

1. Locate a comfortable place where you can comfortably concentrate without any distractions or interruptions.

2. Position yourself in a posture that is alert and relaxed with your back positioned straight.

3. Breath deeply and relax. You can choose to either leave your eyes open or closed. Continue inhaling and exhaling using slow, deep breaths.

4. With your eyes closed, let go of all your problems now as if you are dropping a heavy bag. Know that you are giving yourself this time to detach from external worries.

5. Next, concentrate on your breath. Become totally aware of your sensation of breathing.

6. Begin to count your breaths gently, starting from one and going up to ten, then beginning all over again. If you observe that you missed the sequence before getting to ten, then repeat the process, because this means that you were distracted.

7. Become deeply engrossed in your breathing. Begin to observe the sound, volume,

speed, and warmth of your breath going in and out through your nose.

8. Now, concentrate on the thoughts wandering through your mind, trying to divert your attention away from your breath. Observe them carefully. This step is the most important one.

9. Experience an increased sensation of peace within you as you continue to settle into breathing with more concentration. Take note of how it feels to be in the middle of the fleeting contents of awareness and what it feels like to let them fade away. Notice the calm awareness itself. As soon as you get to this relaxed awareness, you can choose to remain in that state for as long as you desire. Conclude the meditative session by opening your hands, stretching your hands, and standing up.

Your Quick Start Action Step:

1. Write down a list of things that cause you anxiety, worry, and mental stress, and write down why they do so.

2. Now, do a quick meditation or mindfulness practice as highlighted in the chapter

To learn more about freeing your mind from worry, anxiety, and stress, check out "Declutter Your Mind: How to Free Your Thoughts from Worry, Anxiety & Stress Using Mindfulness Techniques for Better Mental Clarity and to Simplify Your Life" by Marie S. Davenport in the online store.

Chapter 9: Decluttering in the Workplace

Chapter 9: Decluttering in the Workplace

Productivity is affected by a decluttered workplace, so clutter should be addressed. We will be discussing this issue in the following chapter.

Why is it Important to Achieve a Clutter-Free Workplace?

You are creating additional space. Office rentals do not come cheap. This option can take up a sizable portion of your business budget. Unfortunately, many businesses retain too much space for irrelevant storage that they do not even need. You should think about getting a document scanning device that will assist in sorting, scanning, and digitizing your files. Some companies also offer the service of shredding redundant documents after converting them to digital versions. There is an incredible method of creating additional space on cabinets, reducing the clutter in storage rooms, and creating significant extra space.

You can also reserve an area or room to store damaged hardware or obsolete equipment that is out of use. You can also make extra cash by recycling or selling outdated hardware that you no longer need. Just try not to allow these items to occupy unnecessary space.

Become organized. Chaos is one of the consequences of a cluttered workplace. You can make your business organized by taking away excess clutter. For example, do you need so many keyboards and mice on your desk? If you have multiple computers or pieces of equipment on one desk, you can create additional space by donating a few of your peripherals to another colleague. Alternatively, you can put up a new desk, or sell them for more money. By doing this, there is additional space on your desk for other relevant things, such as useful documents and letters that may need to be checked. You won't have to look around everywhere to find simple items.

There is no need to look through cabinets or request to borrow things or devices from other members of staff and no more interruptions caused by a disorganized workplace. You can completely concentrate on increasing your productivity in the workplace rather than tidying up the mess created by other people.

Make your working environment as comfortable as possible. Most people prefer working in a quiet and decluttered environment. The secret to increasing productivity is making your workspace free of any distractions or clutter. In addition to promoting positive energy among members of your staff, a well-organized office also makes it easier to work. For instance, you should try to achieve good lighting and use rooms that are soundproof to prevent audio interruptions from outside or nearby offices.

Additionally, decorations like paintings and plants have a calming and relaxing effect on your employees. It lowers their stress levels and uplifts their moods when they must carry out essential tasks.

Making a good impression on clients and new employees. Even if your office is comfortable enough for you and allows you to get the job done, if your office is disorganized, it might drive away customers, potential employees, and clients. To them, the place looks like a total disaster.

If you are concerned about making an excellent first impression, you must organize your office so that it does not look like a mess when an important person visits for a meeting.

In the business world, first impressions matter, so put in a lot of effort to reduce the clutter, organize your workplace, and train your employees to abide by these principles. So when a potential investor visits, there is a higher chance that they will provide funds for your business, rather than telling their friends not to do business with you.

Steps to Declutter Your Workplace

1. Take inventory: Before you begin the process of decluttering your desk, take some time, and make an inventory of your current arrangements. Inspect your desk and its surroundings. Decide on the areas that are included in your workspace that require your attention. These might consist of filing storage, your desk, or anything related to your work that is stored close. Consider also those that are probably in another location or room. Observe the degree of clutter and the overall activity. Get a proper review of what you must handle. Taking physical or mental notes can help you do this.

2. Assess and imagine: Reflect on the periods spent at your desk or workplace and your habits. Are you working from home and all you do is get out of bed, sit on your desk, and check your emails while gobbling breakfast down? Have you fixed your working hours, regardless of whether you are on your desk or not? Do you do things that are not related to work in your area?

Make notes of these things, and assess how beneficial your current habits are to you or if you may need to make modifications to some of them. Imagine your ideal workspace and desk habits. Continue to reflect on this vision in your mind, and allow it to determine your decisions as you move through further steps.

3. Clear up: Take everything away from your desk, and clear out every other storage unit containing your work materials. This step means every single item, including the tiny pictures and post-it notes on your computer. While you are doing this, you can sort everything to these four groups: 1. papers, 2. books, 3.

mementos (items such as pictures that hold memories for you), and 4. other (a collection of other things that do not fit into any group). However, you can create as many subgroups as you like.

4. Clean: Take the bold step, and clean your computer screen, desk, and every other thing. There is a high probability that insects and dirt might have gathered over time, and you may have never had the opportunity to clean your workspace meticulously. There is no better time than now. You might be discouraged initially, but keep in mind that it is more enjoyable to work in an environment that's clean and organized.

5. Change the arrangements: Since everything is clean and empty, consider how beneficial your present arrangement is. You might want to arrange your computer or your desk completely, or perhaps a few of your filing cabinets would be more useful om another position. This opportunity is the best time to make these modifications.

6. Declutter: Now, you must deal with those items you previously placed in those four groups. Look through them in that order, and decide if each object creates a feeling of happiness. Also analyze whether they are supposed to be in your workspace and, most importantly, whether they are vital to your work.

7. Organize: Next, it is time to return the items you would like to keep on your desk and in other storage units. While doing so, keep similar items together, and store a large number of the items in storage units and drawers. Make an effort to keep your desk and other work surfaces as clear as they can be. Additionally, consider how many times you use objects and designate a location for them. What you are trying to achieve is to position all your items in a particular area. This way, you know where everything is located, and it will be easier to return items quickly after each use.

8. Discard: Now that your desk and surrounding areas have been organized, the next thing to do is to deal with those items that do not evoke a positive emotion. Decide on which items to discard, recycle, donate, or return. For instance, borrowed books that must be returned to a friend, colleague, or the library. Then make plans to do just that.

9. Develop new habits: Reflect on your initial objective, and decide whether you want to develop new habits in your personal life and workplace and how to go about it. Additionally, for your desk and workplace to remain decluttered, ensure that you return all items to their particular spaces each day before leaving your workplace.

Your Quick Start Action Step:

1. Assess how disorganized your office desk is.

2. Picture how you want it to look.

3. Now, write the process you intend to follow to get it decluttered, following the steps listed in this chapter.

Chapter 10: Freeing Yourself from Digital Distractions and Clutter

Chapter 10: Freeing Yourself from Digital Distractions and Clutter

Digital clutter reduces the efficiency of the storage capacity of your computer, limiting the storage of your personal data and files. This buildup is why it is necessary to routinely digital declutter to improve the efficiency of your computer. Digital clutter is also a large and mostly unseen killer of productivity. The way you arrange your file folders, browser, and your desktop can easily distract and reduce your productivity. You may not realize how much you are being affected by clutter if your set-up remains unchanged. Distractions such as social media also add to clutter in life and must be dealt with appropriately.

Why It's Important to Deal with Digital Clutter and Distractions

1. **To develop better critical thinking skills:** The brain is likely to become dull and could be overloaded with information when too much time is spent with technology. It is crucial to distance yourself from this

distraction to dive into fresh ideas. These concepts require the use of critical thinking skills that will be hard to develop if you rely too much on technology.

2. **To learn essential skill sets:** Although you might understand a procedure by watching a video, you will never really learn it unless you try it on your own. This action requires you to leave the virtual world and enter into the physical world for actual results. Although technology is a great learning tool, using it to consume content until you get information overload can be distracting. True learning is achieved through practice. You do not only attain knowledge, but you also genuinely learn additional skills when you reduce digital clutter.

3. **To reconnect with or discover new passions:** Digital decluttering helps to increase your free time, allowing you to reconnect to old goals and dreams or to form new ones. Reducing digital clutter will enable you to pursue activities such as run a

marathon, further your education, write a book, or learn an instrument.

4. **To maintain good vision**: Staring at the screen for an extended period can damage the eyes. To maintain good vision, awareness of this is necessary to reduce the time spent on digital activities.

5. **To allow for time to engage the senses:** Digital decluttering will also enable you to have more time to interact with the real world, leading you to enjoy your physical environment. It requires you to cook a meal from scratch, go for a walk, talk to a friend, and learn through experiences.

6. **To stay in shape:** Reducing digital clutter also leads to you taking better care of yourself. Although technologies accurately monitor and time your workout sessions, endeavor that the technology is running in the background. Thirty minutes to an hour is all you need for a good workout per day. Refraining from technology for that period should be done to care for yourself. With time,

you begin to realize that the longer you care for your body, the less you'll rely on technology.

7. **To reconnect with or discover new passions:** Digital decluttering helps you take more interest in the people present in your life. Spending more time with those you love makes it easier for you to stay away from the virtual world.

8. **To become more active socially:** Staying away from the virtual world gets you more opportunities for social activities. This exposure helps improve your interaction with others. This change also leads to others becoming more interesting to you **as a result.**

9. **To allow for more reading time:** Reading improves your communication skills as well as your writing skills. Reading informs and entertains you. Using less technology will enable you to access all of that. Although you can read books on a tablet, the attraction of paper and the weight of a book is difficult to replace. Do not miss out on that by replacing it with mindless scrolling on social media.

10. **To grow in marketability:** Taking advantage of the benefits listed above helps you become more valuable and marketable as an individual, personally, and professionally. It makes you more socially attractive and appealing to others. Also, you have an advantage with potential employers over other job seekers.

How to Digital Declutter

1. Declutter your digital documents.

    • Thoroughly check all your documents, deleting those that are no longer needed.

    • Do not allow the just-in-case syndrome to occur, as you do not need notes from an outdated project, nor do you need the old essays.

    • Peradventure you have many files, arrange them according to their dates and start with the documents that are the oldest. To prevent yourself from getting tired, divide the process into chunks.

2. Organize and delete images.

- Your pictures should be arranged in folders by event or date.

- The pictures should be kept in a cloud drive, such as DropBox or OneDrive, to ensure that you do not need to store them on your computer.

- Photos that are either unimportant or of poor quality should be deleted.

3. Clear out your downloads.

- If you have never cleaned your download folder, it probably takes up a lot of space on your computer.

- To prevent you from being overwhelmed, sort your files according to date, and delete them in bits.

- All the contents in your download folder can be deleted if your important files have already been backed up.

4. Clean up your bookmarks.

- Deleting your bookmarks also helps you to streamline your browser window.

- Bookmarks that aren't needed should be deleted, and those that are necessary can be saved with apps such as Pocket or Evernote.

5. Make a zen desktop.

- As a clean desk also allows one to be more focused and productive, so does having a clean desktop.

- Shortcuts of apps should be removed, and folders and files on the desktop should also be cleaned up.

- Your desktop interface should be made tidier.

- Do not forget to conceal the default taskbar.

6. Delete rarely used accounts.

- Deletion of unnecessary and rarely used accounts helps to prevent time-wasting and reduce the number of passwords to remember.

- Some apps are created to provide a list of sites usually used and how difficult it is to delete your account on each site.

7. Unsubscribe from email lists/newsletters.

- Refrain from thinking that deals and newsletters will be needed later, as they won't be.

- Online shopping deals are the best to unsubscribe from, as they are regular and fill up your inbox.

- If it is necessary to get a newsletter from a particular site, change your email preference to get fewer newsletters. A link is usually placed at the bottom of the newsletters to change your email preferences (although some only offer to unsubscribe).

- For a week or two, open all newsletters you get, and edit your email preferences; this prevents you from being overwhelmed going through your inbox at once.

8. Make sure to defrag/clean your disk.

- This step should be done consistently. If you don't currently do this, check your computer's disk clean options in your computer's settings, and do it immediately. You can find out where it is located on your computer if you do not already know, or ask help from a tech expert.

- Defragging may be scheduled automatically or manually, depending on your OS.

- Third-party apps, such as Disk Space Fan, can also be used.

9. Use automated inbox sorting.

- Your inbox can be programmed to sort your incoming emails if you are making use of Gmail.

- Some apps from a third party can also assist you in sorting your inbox.

10. Unfriend, unfollow, and in general, clean out your social newsfeeds.

- You only get relevant updates when you unfollow people on Twitter. This option enables you to get important news updates on Twitter, be it related to work or personal news. You can also mute anyone you wish to on your Twitter feed.

You will be able to have better access to essential posts on your newsfeed when you unfriend irrelevant people on Facebook. This change will help you to be up-to-date on the activities of your loved ones without spending too much time on the site. Scroll through your list of liked pages and friends and start unfriending.

Your Quick Start Action Step:

1. Write down the ten things that distract you digitally, starting from most to least distracting.

2. Write down how controlling the distractions you get from these gadgets will be beneficial to you.

3. Write down the specific steps you'll take in decluttering your digital life, including a timeframe for each step.

Chapter 11: The Simple Lifestyle

Chapter 11: The Simple Lifestyle

Living life in a simple manner makes life easier. People assume that genuinely living a happy life requires status, shopping for expensive items, gossiping, or other forms of drama, but it only results in dissatisfaction. With a lifestyle that allows you to experience reduced stress and a more relaxed mind, these are some of the advantages of a simple life, depending on the choices you make.

The Keys to Living a Simple Life include:

- **Defining your needs:** Once you understand your needs, you will also realize the things you do not need. Your life naturally becomes simpler.

- **Being intentional:** A powerful way of living your life is by intentional acting and thinking. Once you question yourself on the intentions behind whatever you do, you are actively controlling your life.

- **Understanding your control:** You can only make changes to things within your sphere of influence. You can live a simple life only if you act on things you can control, leaving the things that are not in your control.

Why It's Important to Aim for a Simple Lifestyle

1. **Conscious consumption:** You begin conscious consumption to stop your attachment to addictive use. Living a simple life makes you aware of your spending choices. This mindset makes anything you purchase more valuable. Your awareness of the environmental impact of the consumable goods and the way it sustains a living becomes greater. You make your purchases wisely considering all necessary options.

2. **Achieve more with less:** Living a simple life allows you to have fewer worries, less energy drain, and fewer distractions. You begin to think more explicit, and your life becomes gently paced. You allow more time to understand yourself, which helps you realize and achieve your goals in life. Your energy becomes more focused on fewer and more important goals, which generates better results.

3. **A satisfying lifestyle becomes your priority:** Instead of concentrating on getting more material things, you begin to prioritize for a simpler lifestyle. You start to focus on things that are important to you and not on what the media or other people say. Your lifestyle should be designed to be as meaningful and thoughtful as possible in order to fulfill your inner being.

4. **Your self-worth is no longer connected to the stuff you have accumulated:** You start to take into account more of your self-esteem, and your inspiration for jumping out of bed every morning is not related to the things you acquire. Your soul cannot be satisfied with addictive consumption. You begin to determine the motives that drove you to buy many things and instead focus more on your self-worth.

5. **You now value the gift of time:** Time is seen as a valuable commodity that is better spent by an individual in a more meaningful and relaxed manner. Instead of

having a large home that takes up your time with cleaning, repairing, and maintenance, you should buy a smaller home that saves you energy and time. Time wasters such as watching TV should also be reduced to get a greater sense of value for your time, and you should only work hours befitting your improved lifestyle.

6. **The law of diminishing returns:** The pleasure you derive from experience or having more of something diminishes over time. The first surge of enjoyment felt when purchasing a new item slowly reduces with constant exposure. This shift is usually observed in children filled with excitement at the first experience of owning a toy, but the novelty wears off quickly. Purchasing more things to improve your well-being is not a good long term solution for a more satisfying life.

7. **Your stuff no longer demands your attention:** The things that fill your home continually demands your attention. Energy and time are needed to purchase them in the

first place. Once they get into your homes, you are to decide if they should be cleaned, rearranged, repaired, stored, insured, used, not used, taken out, thought about again, put away, or reorganized into better storage. You also need to decide sometime in the future if you wish to give them away, throw them out, or keep them. This situation leads to a lot of worrying, thinking, energy, and time being channeled on your things, which prevents you from living a simpler lifestyle.

8. **Reduces money stress:** Your money stress is reduced when you live in a smaller but more manageable house that satisfies your needs and helps you save a lot of money. You no longer have to worry about the changes in the mortgage interest rates, and you also spend less money on furniture, cleaning products, heating and cooling, decorations, and things that conform to your finite storage capacity. The family also becomes closer emotionally and physically in a smaller but cozy home.

Minimalist Living

Minimalism is a means of you discovering freedom. This statement could mean freedom from depression, from being overwhelmed, feeling guilty, being worried, or freedom from the consumer culture, which has been made to govern our lives. This is real freedom.

Having material things is not necessarily a bad thing. The problem is that we tend to give a great deal of meaning to our things, often abandoning our passions, personal growth, health, relationships, and our desire to impact others positively. Do you wish to own a big house or brand new car, or do you desire to have a successful career or to raise a family? Choosing the former is relatively not a problem as long as these things really mean something to you. Minimalism simply helps you make your decisions intentionally.

Minimalist living involves a whole new lifestyle. And although having a clutter-free environment is a significant part of it, it includes so much more. Minimalist living also consists in observing the way you spend your money, time, and even how you think.

Living a minimal lifestyle helps you attain happiness, which is what everyone wishes for, right?

Happiness is determined by life itself and not by the things we acquire in life. It is therefore up to you to decide what you need and what is unnecessary in your life.

How to Maintain a Simple Lifestyle

1. **Be kind:** You will not go far in life if the majority does not like you.

2. **Don't criticize:** Whenever you wish to criticize anyone, do not forget that every person does not have access to things you do. Although it is easy to criticize, it is difficult for you to identify if you are criticizing because of boredom, fear, or jealousy.

3. **Don't expect too much:** It is impossible to have your way in all things. It will always seem like something is missing. The point at which you begin to rely on your emotions is the moment you begin to make unfounded assumptions. This attitude makes you lose. Always expect the best and the worst at the same time.

4. **Be present:** Feel the pain while you are exercising. Do not use music to silence it, nor should you ignore the pain. Always live in the moment. You should always be aware of everything you do, feel, and tell yourself. Learn to stay strong through it. Stop making excuses whenever you are feeling discomfort. Use everything you can to learn this.

5. **Dealing with idiots, arrogance, and the like:** We live in an ecosystem of largely crazy individuals. Some people out there wake up and walk in the same crap daily, rather than stepping around it or clearing it from their lane. They castigate everyone aside from themselves.

6. **Tell yourself a different story:** When whatever's being said does not sit well with you, start your own discourse.

7. **Redefine everything in your life:** Odds are you've heard all sorts of lies about being successful, influential, and living the best life. Being successful has been predefined as finishing college, landing a great job, getting a

good car, having a wonderful body, etc. These things are necessarily not equivalent to real success for everyone, and they do not need to be. The American Dream might play out well for others but not work for you.

Redefine success for yourself: Reevaluate the meaning of life to you. Reexamine the beliefs that were ingrained in you to make you follow someone else's vision and keep you playing it safe in life. Immediately after you find out what you really want, go out and make it happen.

8. **Ask why:** Question yourself on why you do the things you do. If getting a relevant answer becomes a problem for you, then you should likely not do it. For instance, I had a Facebook account and had about 700 friends, with around 10 of them being my actual friends. Still, I kept on logging onto this virtual world for no substantial reason. I would monitor the lives of others and concentrate on them rather than focus on myself, my work, and my real friends. Bring clarity to the reasons

you do the things you do and if there is a genuine intent to back it. Question yourself about ways you can be better.

9. **Focus on you:** Stop fixating and getting bothered about how other people live their lives. Life gets better when you learn to close off the outside noise and concentrate more on yourself.

Your Quick Start Action Step:

1. Write down the three most crucial things that you want your life to revolve around.

2. Analyze your life as it is. Jot down what you do daily, who you spend your time with, what your expenses are, what your place of abode is, and every other thing you can think of. How do they all back your values, and how do they work with these values?

3. Go over everything you wrote down, and eliminate what does not back

your values and what you do not want in your happier life. Discard the regret and liabilities, and concentrate on the things that make you happy.

4. Write out what you would like to include in your life to better back your values. In what ways are they suitable for your new life? This task can be more straightforward if done on a computer, as you can simply move things around.

5. Take note of a minute thing you can do to be a step closer to your happier and more comfortable life. Transform your diet one meal at a time. Leave a group that's not contributing to your development anymore. Begin to walk more. Remain around people that use up your energy less. Clear a cluttered area in your life, whether it be emotionally or physically.

6. Every time you take a step regarding

your new life, pause and contemplate how you feel. Is it benefiting you or do you need to change something about it?

7. Decide to dwell intimately with your brand new life daily, and keep cultivating new habits

8. Carry out an action that backs up your values. You can do this activity every day, and ensure you take time to observe how it feels inside. As you adhere to the process, these small things would eventually add up in helping you become a better version of yourself.

Bonus Chapter: Planning Family Recreational Activities

Bonus Chapter: Planning Family Recreational Activities

An increasing number of employees do not even use their vacation leave anymore. Tasks like work, school, screen time, extracurricular activities, and daily routines draw families in separate directions. Coming together can be like herding cats. Arranging a calendar must be deliberate, and it depends on the unity and engagement of all the members of the family.

Decluttering your life is more than arranging and clearing your physical space. It needs a deliberate technique to plan your time and set up activities with your family. Decluttering one's life also makes room for more fun and recreation. It has been proven that more recreation time reduces stress, which we want to reduce or eliminate, whenever possible. New research4).

Why It's Important to Plan for Recreational Activities

_____

- **Everyone needs a break:** The daily routine burns us out, and most times, a vacation is one of the ways to get away and ignore work and a tight schedule. A vacation can help you unwind and forget about the stress of your daily life, and it should be cheerful and fun. When you take a vacation, you come back invigorated, and you become a better employee, a better spouse, and a better parent.

- **Lasting memories:** Kids enjoy going through scrapbooks where your memories of your family vacation are documented. They will discuss their adventures, such as the things they've seen and the fun they had on the leaves. These are memories they will share with their children someday, and this is important. Your kids will know that you loved being with them and spending time with them through these family vacations.

- **Open your eyes:** Going on vacation with your kids will open them up to new people and new cultures, which is a good thing. Even if you do not go outside of your home country, your children can learn about the local cuisines from you, the history of the region, and learn about locations and activities. Help them understand that the world is their classroom.

- **Reconnect:** Vacations strengthen relationships and family ties. Carrying out activities that are not part of what you usually do and leaving your comfort zone will help strengthen you as an individual and your family.

- **It's about time:** A vacation is us time, with no emails to read, laundry to fold, or bathrooms to scrub. You can concentrate on each other doing whatever you want to, even if it's just lying on the beach and watching your kids play in the sand. Does that not sound great?

Steps for Planning a Recreational Activity

1. Get a calendar for the period you want to plan for. It is excellent to have it printed out. I recommended planning for the future; if possible, at least, prepare for a month. The real

advantage of this is seen when you plan for a whole season (about 3-6 months out). This approach works because taking an extensive view of your family responsibilities and reviewing your checklist will ensure your calendar is not packed. This assessment leaves room for flexibility and increases the probability that your family will do all the fun things they have planned.

2. Write out all your family's already planned responsibilities:

- Birthday parties. If a birthday party you just cannot miss is coming up, you can modestly buzz the parents and ask when they're planning the party, so you do not miss it).

- Church events

- Sports practices and games

- Planned travel/vacations

- Out of town guest visits

3. Take inventory of your family's rhythms,

personality needs, etc.:

- Do your kids need to nap?

- What are your kids' bedtimes?

- What is your budget?

- When do you need to do your grocery shopping or do laundry?

- Are there any special adult events coming up?

- What balance do you want between scheduled activities and free play?

- What are the pockets of time you have?

4. Let Google be your friend. You can even check Facebook for where and when the best adventures are happening.

- Major special events (something that happens only once in a year)

- Special events for the local area (annual events, a special parade, etc.)

- Special events for a venue
- Seasonal (Christmas lights, Easter eggs, strawberry picking season, fall festivals)
- A mix of activities
  - Day-long trips
  - Half-day trips
  - Easy and quick trips (1-2 hours)
  - City stuff
  - Fairs and festivals
  - Amusement parks
  - Parks and playgrounds
  - Museums
  - Nature centers
  - Indoor activities
  - Outdoor activities

5. Create a bucket list of family fun activities and set it up:

- Include the whole family in this process. Acknowledge the desires and needs of everyone in the family.

- Arrange in order of priority, so you do not miss an activity or event.

6. Put the planned-out draft of activities into the fun schedule of your family. Don't try to fit everything in (it won't work!).

7. Ensure there's room for flexibility in your schedule. Be mindful of the activities that only occur once in a year or a season and the ones that are "Plug and Play", which can be plugged in anywhere.

- Put in backup days for the vital activities.

- If there's rain, what can be moved around?

- If any unplanned things occur, how can these opportunities be fit in?

- What if someone gets sick?

8. Build-in downtimes:

- Weekly downtime

- Monthly downtime. Designate at least one weekend where you are not all that busy. This approach doesn't mean you can't schedule anything, but that not every weekend can be a comprehensive trip to Six Flags or any amusement park.

9. Look into creating more special days aside from weekends. If you can manipulate your work schedule to take time off during the week, this will boost your family's fun plan. I make time during the week sometimes (because there are fewer people) to carry out activities like:

- Checking out the tulip fields or sunflower fields

- Doing something special like going to an amusement park or a special beach

- Strawberry picking

10. Divide and conquer. You all do not have

to go for everything as a family. Let yourself have some adult time, and bring a trustworthy adult along.

Your Quick Start Action Step:

Refer to the section "Steps on planning a recreational activity", and plan the steps discussed.

Conclusion

Thank you again for owning this book!

Decluttering your life can be a natural process that could lead you to a better and healthier lifestyle. It may require daily, time-to-time consciousness of your environment, dwelling, and state of mind. But achieving it is definitely doable, especially if it meets your personal goals.

Without intervention, your workplace and home would sway from place to place, becoming chaotic in pursuit of distractions. When you refuse to take care of your clutter, your being and dwelling will remain chaotic. Due to this, your life experiences will be variable and utterly reliant on the haphazard nature of things.

The chaos experienced in diverse aspects of your life depicts the annoying truth that many of the current systems are not under our deliberate control. To make matters worse, this chaos feels very concrete and robust, and they have an intense effect on our capacity and view of our surroundings.

In spite of all this, let the paralyzing feeling brought about by clutter go.

Even if your subconscious mind doesn't let you have total control over your nature, you have the power to handle many of them. You still can adjust so that you can control your clutter-developing tendencies.

Contained throughout this book is a comprehensive collection of insights and tools for decluttering your life. Thus, this book has provided you with tips that you could apply to the various facets of your life to achieve beneficial results for your lifestyle and general well being. These techniques would not only improve your life and reduce your stress levels but also give you that peace of mind.

Any necessary process requires patience, but the outcome is always worth it. However, before you start making any life-changing decisions, remember the importance of changing your mindset first. The truth is that we have varied mindsets at various times. Mindset is the outstanding shared characteristic successful people have. They have the correct attitude towards decluttering.

As you assess your fundamental values, you can then devise a plan for your decisions and actions. By doing so, you don't give yourself reasons to overthink and even worry.

Once your life priorities are clear, you do not squander your time on things that will cause you to regret or give you mental distress in the future.

You set the stage for targeted action and self-esteem that keeps you invigorated when your goals are established on your priorities and values.

When you set out and live your zeal, you saturate your goals with credibility, joy, and purpose with little or no room for pessimism.

By being more present and attentive in your relationships, you avoid most of the discord that comes with communicating with them. This step also reduces the emotional suffering that will come about and then maximizing contentment with the relationship.

By keeping your home and digital world clean, arranged, and streamlined, you take away distractions that prevent you from reaching your goals, priorities, and values.

By deciding to reduce your chores and obligations, you decrease your stress, hence allowing more time to be in the moment and to be more mindful of life.

When you concentrate on the job at hand at home and engage yourself into these decluttering endeavors, you fix the clutter in your dwelling to synchronize with the activity, promoting a sensation of great happiness and deep satisfaction. As you deal with procrastination and swiftly take the fundamental steps, you sidestep the tension that accompanies procrastinating and finish off the tasks.

By being attentive to the daily activities of life, from regular dishwashing to working out, you erase your mind out of everything else except on what is important - the present.

Outline your fundamental values, life preferences, and goals. When you have these personalized structures in place, it will be easier for you to ascertain where you have the most upsetting clutter and how you want to handle it.

All the practices stated in this book can be utilized

for a brief amount of time daily. The outcome of these practices will help you with complicated ventures, such as bettering the organization of your home, time, family, and relationship, and discovering your passion or defeating the past.

Keep a journal where you write down the declutter practices you carry out and the changes seen in your life as a result. By tracking your actions and the outcomes, you'll feel encouraged to continue with your decluttering exercise.

Decluttering is a lifelong process that pays great rewards that can markedly affect your quality of life. The lesser time spent with meddlesome clutter in your life, the additional time you'll have to savor the present moment.

You have what it takes to achieve the lifestyle that you deserve and fix the things that clutter your life, so take charge now. Start now with the most substantial clutter in your life to begin this process today.

Thank you and best of luck!

References

Decluttering Doesn't Work | The Minimalists. (2019). Retrieved from https://www.theminimalists.com/decluttering/

News, A. (2019). Einstein Was Right: Clutter Is Good. Retrieved from https://abcnews.go.com/Technology/tidy-messy-environment-impact-decisions-behavior-study/story?id=19909678

Liu, J., Smeesters, D., & Trampe, D. (2012). RETRACTED: Effects of Messiness on Preferences for Simplicity. Journal Of Consumer Research, 39(1), 199-214. doi: 10.1086/662139

Hoarding Disorders UK (2019). Retrieved from https://hoardingdisordersuk.org/wp-content/uploads/2014/01/clutter-image-ratings.pdf

5 Surprising Reasons Why Spring Cleaning is Good for You [LIST] - Goodnet. (2019). Retrieved from https://www.goodnet.org/articles/5-surprising-reasons-spring-cleaning-good-for-you-list

Time Off and Vacation Usage. (2019). Retrieved from https://www.ustravel.org/toolkit/time-and-vacation-usage

Green, M., & Rosenfeld, L. (2014). Breathing Room: Open Your Heart by Decluttering Your Home. Simon and Schuster.

Johnson, B. (2013). Zero waste home: The ultimate guide to simplifying your life by reducing your waste. Simon and Schuster.

Desmarais, R. (2016). Time for spring cleaning and decluttering? But what about books?. The Deakin Review of Children's Literature, 5(4).

Harriet, S. (2005). Unclutter your life: is clutter creating chaos for you? Learn simple ways to declutter your home. IDEA Fitness Journal, 2(2), 94-96.

Bigelow, D. (2014). Clear the Clutter, Find Happiness: One-Minute Tips for Decluttering and Refreshing Your Home and Your Life.

Williamson, G. A. (2017). The Home Decluttering Diet: Organize Your Way to a Clean and Lean House.

Fitzmartin, C. (2003). Home with Fun: Ten Steps

to Turn Your Home Into a Fun Place to Live!. iUniverse.

www.ingramcontent.com/pod-product-compliance
Lightning Source LLC
Chambersburg PA
CBHW071228070526
44583CB00017B/2085